The Power Within

Unlocking Your Potential for Personal Growth and Success

Written By:

April Angelli Hildred

Copyright

© 2024 by April Angelli Hildred

This book is a work of the author's own research and reflections. It is intended to provide helpful and informative material on the subjects addressed. The author and publisher specifically disclaim any responsibility for liability, loss, or risk incurred as a direct or indirect consequence of the use and application of any of the contents in this book.

Dedication

To my Papa, Brother's, Sister's in law, Tito's, Tita's and Cousins: Your love and support have been the steady foundation upon which I've built my life. Thank you for always believing in me and for nurturing my dreams. Every step of this journey has been a tribute to the values you've instilled in me.

To my husband, Lee: You are my constant rock and unwavering champion. Through every doubt and challenge, your belief in me has never wavered. Your encouragement has been the heartbeat behind every page, and your love has given me the strength to press forward. I am endlessly grateful for your steadfast support, for every moment you lifted me up, and for pushing me to see my own potential. This book would not exist without you by my side.

To all my dear friends, especially to Julia, Khusbu, Mary, Maud, Victoria, Maria, Emma, Marilyn, Shaniya, Eleni, Iris, Amalor, Hazel, Georlin and Lorraine: You each bring light, laughter, and strength to my life. Your friendship has been a source of joy and inspiration, filling my world with shared dreams, day or night conversations, and countless memories that have shaped who I am. Thank you for your unwavering belief in me, for standing by me, and for always cheering me on. You have each, in your own way, fuelled this journey, and your presence in my life is cherished beyond words.

This book is dedicated to all of you, with heartfelt gratitude.

April Angelli Hildred

Table of Contents

Introduction

In a world that is constantly changing and evolving, the quest for personal growth and success has become more important than ever. Each of us is born with immense potential, yet the journey to realising that potential is often fraught with challenges, distractions, and obstacles. **"The Power Within: Unlocking Your Potential for Personal Growth and Success"** is a guide for anyone who desires to tap into their inner strength, break free from limiting beliefs, and live a life of purpose, fulfillment, and achievement.

Understanding Personal Growth

Personal growth is a lifelong journey that encompasses all areas of life, including emotional, mental, physical, spiritual, and financial well-being. It's the process of striving to become the best version of yourself, to develop new skills, acquire knowledge, build resilience, and expand your horizons. Unlike many other endeavours in life that have a clear endpoint, personal growth is an ongoing evolution. There's always something more to learn, more to experience, and more ways to grow.

The key to personal growth lies in recognising that the power to change and succeed resides within you. The world may offer tools, advice, and opportunities, but it is your mindset, your actions, and your commitment that will determine the direction and quality of your life. This book explores the profound impact of self-awareness, resilience, discipline, and action, all of which are necessary to unlock your potential.

The Gap Between Potential and Reality

Every individual possesses untapped potential. However, for many, there remains a significant gap between the potential they hold and the reality they experience. Why is it that some people seem to achieve their goals effortlessly while others struggle to make progress? Why do so many people feel stuck, overwhelmed, or unsure of how to move forward?

The answers lie in the way we think, feel, and act. Fear, procrastination, limiting beliefs, lack of focus, and external pressures often prevent us from realising our potential. We may know deep down that we are capable of more, but we become trapped in patterns of behaviour that hold us back. This book is designed to help you break through those barriers, overcome the mental and emotional obstacles that stand in your way, and unlock the power within you to achieve the success you desire.

Why This Book?

The motivation for writing "The Power Within: Unlocking Your Potential for Personal Growth and Success" comes from a deep understanding of the struggles many individuals face in their pursuit of personal and professional fulfillment. In today's fast-paced world, where external pressures and distractions abound, it's easy to lose sight of what truly matters. Many people find themselves caught in the grind of daily life, disconnected from their passions and unable to see a clear path to their goals. This book aims to provide not just inspiration, but practical, actionable strategies that anyone can implement to begin transforming their life.

Whether you're just starting your journey of personal development, or you've been on the path for a while, this book is structured to meet you where you are. The insights, techniques, and tools presented in each chapter are designed to help you become more self-aware, increase your emotional intelligence, improve your productivity, and cultivate resilience—all of which are vital for unlocking your potential.

Key Themes of the Book

"The Power Within" covers a wide range of topics essential for personal growth and success. The following key themes are explored in detail throughout the book:

1. Self-Awareness: Personal growth begins with self-awareness. Understanding your strengths, weaknesses, values, and motivations is the foundation upon which you can build a life that aligns with your true self. This book delves into the importance of introspection and provides exercises for increasing self-awareness.

2. Resilience and Grit: Life is full of challenges, setbacks, and disappointments. Developing resilience—the ability to bounce back from adversity—is crucial for long-term success. The book also explores the concept of grit, which is the combination of passion and perseverance that drives individuals to pursue their long-term goals, even in the face of obstacles.

3. Goal Setting and Action: One of the most important aspects of personal growth is setting clear, achievable goals and taking consistent action toward them. The book outlines effective goal-setting techniques and emphasises the importance of turning knowledge into action.

4. Mindset: Your mindset shapes your reality. A growth mindset—the belief that you can develop your abilities through effort and learning—is a key ingredient for success. This book teaches you how to shift from a fixed mindset to a growth mindset, allowing you to embrace challenges and persist in the face of setbacks.

5. Emotional Intelligence: Success is not just about intellectual intelligence (IQ); emotional intelligence (EQ) plays an equally important role. Understanding and managing your emotions, as well as building empathy and strong social connections, are critical for both personal and professional success.

6. Overcoming Procrastination and Perfectionism: Procrastination and perfectionism are two of the most common obstacles to personal growth. This book provides strategies for overcoming these self-sabotaging behaviours and replacing them with productive habits.

7. Health and Wellness: True success cannot be achieved without taking care of your body and mind. This book emphasises the importance of holistic wellness, including the mind-body connection, physical fitness, nutrition, and mental health.

8. Financial Management: Financial stability and success are key components of overall well-being. This book offers practical advice on managing your finances, building wealth, and achieving financial independence.

9. Taking Action and Implementing Change: Ultimately, knowledge without action is useless. This book provides a roadmap for turning your goals into reality, overcoming the fear of taking action, and staying committed to long-term change.

A Roadmap to Unlocking Your Potential

The structure of this book is designed to guide you step-by-step through the process of unlocking your potential. Each chapter builds on the previous one, creating a comprehensive roadmap to personal growth and success. You will find that the chapters are filled with practical exercises, reflective questions, and actionable strategies that encourage you to take control of your own development.

• Chapter 1 starts by defining self-help and its benefits, setting the stage for the transformative journey ahead.

• In Chapter 2, we explore the role of self-awareness in personal growth, emphasising how critical it is to understand yourself before attempting to change your life.

• Chapter 3 focuses on goal setting, helping you clarify what you want to achieve and why.

• Throughout the subsequent chapters, we delve deeper into the psychological, emotional, and practical tools you need to overcome obstacles, develop resilience, and maintain momentum.

By the time you reach the final chapters, you will have a clear understanding of what it takes to achieve long-term growth and success. You'll be equipped with the tools to manage stress, improve your relationships, build financial independence, and ultimately, lead a life that is fulfilling and aligned with your values.

Who This Book Is For

This book is for anyone who wants to take control of their life and unlock their potential. Whether you're feeling stuck, overwhelmed, or uncertain about your future, "The Power Within" will provide you with the tools and strategies to break through your limitations and achieve the success you desire. It's for:

• Students and professionals looking to enhance their personal and professional skills.

• Individuals in transition whether you're facing a career change, personal challenges, or a new life phase, this book will help you navigate those transitions with confidence.

• Entrepreneurs and leaders who want to improve their emotional intelligence, build resilience, and create a growth-oriented mindset.

• Anyone who feels they have untapped potential and is ready to take action toward living their best life.

A Call to Action

The power to transform your life resides within you. You are not limited by your past, your circumstances, or your current challenges. By embracing the principles outlined in this book, you will discover the limitless potential you possess. Remember that personal growth is not a linear process; it's a journey of learning, evolving, and expanding. There will be setbacks along the way, but with persistence, resilience, and the right tools, you can overcome any obstacle.

As you read through the pages of this book, take time to reflect on your own life and the changes you want to make. Implement the strategies, apply the lessons, and most importantly, take action. The road to success is paved with effort, consistency, and self-belief.

"The Power Within: Unlocking Your Potential for Personal Growth and Success" is more than just a book, it's an invitation to begin your journey of self-discovery, to unlock your true potential, and to create the life you've always dreamed of.

Are you ready to unlock the power within?

Chapter 1: Defining Self-Help and Its Benefits

1.1 What is Self-Help?

Self-help is a journey of personal empowerment, where individuals take the initiative to improve their lives by addressing challenges, setting goals, and enhancing their well-being. Unlike relying solely on external sources like therapy or counselling, self-help emphasises personal responsibility and the proactive pursuit of growth. This concept is deeply rooted in the belief that everyone has the potential to overcome obstacles and create a fulfilling life, using the right tools, strategies, and mindset. Understanding the foundation of self-help, its historical context, and its modern applications provides insight into why it has become a powerful force for change in today's world.

The Concept of Self-Help

Self-help, as a concept, refers to the practice of taking personal responsibility for improving one's own life, particularly in the areas of emotional well-being, mental health, personal development, and professional growth. It is the idea that individuals can actively take steps to improve their lives, using various tools, strategies, and resources to become the best versions of themselves. At its core, self-help is about empowerment, giving people the knowledge, skills, and motivation to make positive changes in their lives without relying solely on external assistance.

The concept of self-help is rooted in the belief that individuals have the power to change their circumstances, no matter how difficult they may seem. It emphasises personal agency, autonomy, and the importance of self-determination. By engaging in self-help practices, people can work towards overcoming challenges, achieving their goals, and improving their overall quality of life.

Self-help is not limited to one particular area of life. It can encompass everything from managing stress and anxiety to building self-confidence, improving relationships, and achieving financial stability. The beauty of self-help lies in its flexibility that can be tailored to suit the unique needs and goals of each individual.

Historical Perspectives on Self-Help

The roots of self-help can be traced back to ancient times, when philosophers, religious leaders, and thinkers offered guidance on how to live a virtuous and fulfilling life. For example, the teachings of Confucius in ancient China emphasised the importance of self-cultivation and personal responsibility. Similarly, in ancient Greece, philosophers like Socrates, Plato, and Aristotle explored the concept of self-improvement through the pursuit of knowledge, virtue, and self-discipline.

In the Western world, the idea of self-help gained prominence during the 19th century with the publication of Samuel Smiles book Self-Help, which is often regarded as the foundational text of the modern self-help movement. Published in 1859, Smiles book encouraged readers to take control of their own lives through hard work, perseverance, and self-discipline. His famous quote, "Heaven helps those who help themselves," encapsulates the essence of the self-help philosophy.

During the 20th century, the self-help movement continued to evolve, with the rise of psychology and the emergence of various self-help genres, including books, seminars, and support groups. Pioneers such as Dale Carnegie, with his book How to Win Friends and Influence People, and Napoleon Hill, with Think and Grow Rich, further popularised the concept of self-help by focusing on personal development, success, and positive thinking.

The late 20th and early 21st centuries saw an explosion of self-help resources, fuelled by advances in technology and the increasing demand for personal growth. The rise of the internet, social media, and online platforms has made self-help more accessible than ever, allowing people from all walks of life to engage with self-help content and communities.

Modern Self-Help: Trends and Movements

In the modern era, self-help has become a multi-billion-dollar industry, encompassing a wide range of products and services, including books, podcasts, online courses, workshops, and coaching. The self-help genre has expanded to cover various aspects of life, from health and wellness to career success, relationships, and spirituality.

One of the most significant trends in modern self-help is the focus on mental health and emotional well-being. With the growing awareness of the importance of mental health, more people are turning to self-help resources to manage stress, anxiety, depression, and other emotional challenges. Mindfulness, meditation, and cognitive-behavioural techniques have become popular tools for individuals seeking to improve their mental health.

Another trend in modern self-help is the emphasis on holistic well-being, which recognises the interconnectedness of physical, mental, emotional, and spiritual health. Many self-help resources now advocate for a balanced approach to life, encouraging individuals to prioritise self-care, healthy habits, and personal growth in all areas of their lives.

The rise of social media influencers and online communities has also played a significant role in shaping modern self-help. Influencers who share their personal stories of growth and transformation have inspired millions of followers to embark on their own self-help journeys. Online communities provide a supportive environment where individuals can connect with like-minded people, share their experiences, and receive encouragement.

Moreover, the concept of self-help has expanded to include social and collective well-being. Many modern self-help movements emphasise the importance of community, social justice, and environmental sustainability. This shift reflects a growing recognition that personal growth is not just about individual success but also about contributing to the greater good.

1.2 The Benefits of Self-Help

The self-help movement offers numerous benefits, ranging from personal growth and transformation to enhanced emotional and mental well-being. At its core, self-help empowers individuals to take control of their lives, making deliberate choices to improve various aspects of their existence. Whether it's developing a growth mindset, managing stress, or cultivating resilience, self-help provides the tools needed to navigate life's challenges. By exploring these benefits in detail, you'll gain a deeper understanding of how self-help can significantly enhance life satisfaction, personal fulfillment, and overall well-being.

Personal Growth and Transformation

One of the most significant benefits of self-help is the potential for personal growth and transformation. Engaging in self-help practices allows individuals to identify areas of their lives that need improvement and take actionable steps to create positive change. Whether it's developing new skills, overcoming limiting beliefs, or breaking unhealthy habits, self-help empowers people to become the best versions of themselves.

Personal growth through self-help often involves a deep level of self-awareness and reflection. By examining one's thoughts, behaviours, and emotions, individuals can gain insight into their patterns and triggers. This self-awareness is the first step towards making meaningful changes and achieving personal goals.

The process of personal growth through self-help is often incremental. Small, consistent efforts can lead to significant transformations over time. For example, practicing gratitude daily can lead to a more positive outlook on life, while setting and achieving small goals can build confidence and motivation for larger challenges.

Personal transformation through self-help is not just about achieving external success; it's also about inner growth. Many self-help practices encourage individuals to cultivate qualities such as resilience, compassion, and patience. As people grow internally, they often find that their external circumstances improve as well.

Emotional and Mental Well-Being

Another crucial benefit of self-help is the enhancement of emotional and mental well-being. In today's fast-paced and often stressful world, many people struggle with anxiety, depression, and other mental health challenges. Self-help offers tools and strategies to manage these issues and improve overall emotional health.

One of the most effective self-help practices for emotional well-being is mindfulness. Mindfulness involves paying attention to the present moment without judgment, which can help reduce stress and increase emotional regulation. Meditation, deep breathing exercises, and journaling are other self-help techniques that promote emotional health.

Self-help can also play a significant role in improving mental well-being by addressing negative thought patterns and cognitive distortions. Cognitive-behavioural techniques, such as reframing negative thoughts, can help individuals develop a more positive and realistic outlook on life. Additionally, self-help practices that promote self-compassion and self-acceptance can reduce feelings of shame, guilt, and self-criticism.

Furthermore, self-help resources often provide valuable information and guidance on managing specific mental health issues, such as anxiety, depression, and stress. By empowering individuals with knowledge and practical strategies, self-help can complement professional mental health treatment and support individuals in their healing journey.

Enhancing Life Satisfaction and Fulfillment

Ultimately, the goal of self-help is to enhance life satisfaction and fulfillment. By taking proactive steps to improve various aspects of life, individuals can create a more meaningful and fulfilling existence. Whether it's achieving personal goals, building stronger relationships, or finding purpose, self-help can lead to a greater sense of contentment and happiness.

One of the ways self-help enhances life satisfaction is by helping individuals align their actions with their values and priorities. When people live in accordance with their true selves, they are more likely to experience a sense of fulfillment and purpose. Self-help practices, such as goal setting and values clarification, can help individuals identify what truly matters to them and take steps to create a life that reflects their values.

In addition to personal fulfillment, self-help can also improve relationships and social connections. Many self-help resources focus on communication skills, empathy, and conflict resolution, which can lead to stronger and more meaningful relationships. As individuals grow and develop through self-help, they often find that their relationships with others also improve.

Moreover, self-help encourages individuals to take ownership of their lives and make choices that lead to greater happiness and well-being. This sense of agency and empowerment can significantly enhance life satisfaction, as people feel more in control of their destiny and more capable of creating the life they desire.

1.3 The Self-Help Journey

Embarking on a self-help journey is both an exciting and challenging endeavour. It begins with a decision to take control of one's life and make meaningful changes. However, starting this journey can sometimes be met with resistance, doubts, or fears. The key to success lies in setting realistic expectations, being patient with oneself, and embracing the process of growth. This section delves into the initial steps of the self-help journey, addressing common obstacles and offering guidance on how to stay committed and motivated. Through small, consistent actions, individuals can transform their lives and achieve lasting personal growth.

Starting Your Self-Help Journey

The decision to embark on a self-help journey is often the result of a desire for change. Whether it's improving one's mental health, achieving personal goals, or finding greater meaning in life, the first step in the self-help journey is recognising the need for change and taking action.

Starting a self-help journey can be both exciting and intimidating. The prospect of personal growth and transformation is inspiring, but it can also be overwhelming to know where to begin. The key is to start small and take incremental steps towards your goals. For example, if your goal is to improve your mental health, you might begin by practicing mindfulness for a few minutes each day or journaling your thoughts and feelings.

Another important aspect of starting your self-help journey is setting realistic expectations. Personal growth takes time, and it's essential to be patient with yourself as you navigate the process. It's also important to recognise that setbacks and challenges are a natural part of the journey. The key is to stay committed and keep moving forward, even when progress seems slow.

In addition to taking small steps and setting realistic expectations, it's also helpful to seek out resources and support as you begin your self-help journey. There are countless self-help books, podcasts, online courses, and communities available to guide and inspire you. Finding resources that resonate with you can provide valuable guidance and motivation as you embark on your journey.

Overcoming Initial Resistance

It's not uncommon to encounter resistance when starting a self-help journey. This resistance can take many forms, such as self-doubt, fear of failure, or a lack of motivation. Overcoming this resistance is a crucial part of the self-help process.

One of the most effective ways to overcome resistance is to acknowledge and address the underlying fears and limiting beliefs that may be holding you back. For example, if you're afraid of failure, it can be helpful to remind yourself that failure is a natural part of the learning process and an opportunity for growth. Reframing negative thoughts and beliefs can help reduce resistance and increase motivation.

Another strategy for overcoming resistance is to break your goals down into smaller, more manageable tasks. When a goal feels too big or overwhelming, it's easy to feel stuck or unmotivated. By breaking the goal down into smaller steps, you can create a sense of progress and momentum, which can help reduce resistance.

It's also important to practice self-compassion as you navigate resistance. It's normal to encounter challenges and setbacks on your self-help journey, and it's essential to be kind to yourself when things don't go as planned. Self-compassion can help reduce feelings of shame and guilt, which can often contribute to resistance.

Lastly, surrounding yourself with a supportive community can also help you overcome resistance. Whether it's joining a self-help group, working with a coach, or connecting with like-minded individuals online, having a support system can provide encouragement, accountability, and motivation to keep going.

Setting Expectations and Embracing the Process

Setting realistic expectations and embracing the process are essential components of a successful self-help journey. Personal growth is not a linear process, and it's important to be patient and flexible as you navigate the ups and downs.

One of the most common challenges people face on their self-help journey is the desire for quick results. It's natural to want to see immediate progress, but it's essential to recognise that lasting change takes time. Setting realistic expectations about the timeline for achieving your goals can help you stay committed and avoid frustration.

Embracing the process also means being open to experimentation and learning. Not every self-help strategy will work for everyone, and it's essential to be willing to try different approaches and adapt as needed. For example, if one mindfulness technique doesn't resonate with you, it's okay to try another until you find what works best.

Another aspect of embracing the process is recognising that setbacks and challenges are a natural part of the journey. Personal growth often involves stepping outside of your comfort zone and facing difficult emotions or situations. It's important to approach these challenges with curiosity and compassion, rather than judgment or frustration.

Finally, celebrating your progress and successes along the way is crucial for maintaining motivation and a positive mindset. Whether it's achieving a small goal, overcoming a challenge, or simply sticking with your self-help practices, taking the time to acknowledge and celebrate your progress can help reinforce your commitment to the journey.

Chapter 2: The Power of Positive Thinking

Positive thinking is more than just a feel-good concept; it is a powerful tool that can transform your life. The idea that maintaining a positive outlook can influence outcomes is rooted in both psychology and real-world experience. Positive thinking involves focusing on the good in any situation and maintaining an optimistic attitude, even in the face of challenges. This chapter explores the nature of positive thinking, its scientific underpinnings, and how you can develop a positive mindset to improve various aspects of your life. By understanding and embracing the power of positive thinking, you can unlock new opportunities for personal growth, enhance your mental and emotional health, and build stronger, more fulfilling relationships.

2.1 Understanding Positive Thinking

Positive thinking is a foundational element of self-help and personal development. It is a mental and emotional attitude that focuses on the bright side of life and expects positive results. While it may seem like a simplistic approach, the effects of positive thinking are far-reaching and well-supported by scientific research. Understanding what positive thinking is, how it works, and its impact on daily life is crucial for harnessing its power.

What is Positive Thinking?

At its core, positive thinking is the practice of focusing on the good in any given situation. It involves having an optimistic outlook, expecting positive outcomes, and maintaining hope even in difficult times. Positive thinking is not about ignoring reality or denying challenges, but rather about approaching life's obstacles with a mindset that emphasises potential solutions and opportunities for growth.

Positive thinking is a mindset that can be cultivated over time. It requires a conscious effort to reframe negative thoughts and replace them with more constructive and empowering beliefs. For example, instead of viewing a setback as a failure, a positive thinker might see it as an opportunity to learn and improve. This shift in perspective can have a profound impact on how individuals perceive and respond to challenges.

While positive thinking often begins with self-talk—the internal dialogue that shapes our perception of reality—it extends to how we interpret external events. A positive thinker tends to look for the silver lining in situations, believing that even adverse circumstances can lead to positive outcomes. This approach not only influences how we feel about the world around us but also impacts our actions and behaviours.

The Science Behind Positive Thinking

The concept of positive thinking is supported by a growing body of scientific research that highlights its effects on the brain and overall well-being. Studies in psychology and neuroscience have shown that positive thinking can rewire the brain, leading to improved mental and emotional health.

One of the key findings in this area is the impact of positive thinking on neuroplasticity—the brain's ability to change and adapt over time. When individuals engage in positive thinking, they strengthen neural pathways associated with optimism, resilience, and well-being. This can lead to lasting changes in how they perceive and respond to the world.

Positive thinking is also linked to the production of neurotransmitters such as serotonin and dopamine, which are associated with feelings of happiness and well-being. When we think positively, our brain releases these chemicals, creating a feedback loop that reinforces positive emotions and reduces stress.

Moreover, research has shown that positive thinking can improve immune function, reduce the risk of chronic diseases, and increase longevity. This is partly because positive thinkers tend to engage in healthier behaviours, such as regular exercise, balanced eating, and stress management practices. Additionally, a positive mindset can buffer the effects of stress by promoting adaptive coping mechanisms and reducing the body's physiological response to stressors.

The Impact of Positive Thoughts on Daily Life

The influence of positive thinking extends beyond the brain and body; it also shapes our daily experiences and interactions. When we approach life with a positive mindset, we are more likely to notice opportunities, take proactive steps toward our goals, and build stronger relationships.

In daily life, positive thinking can help us navigate challenges with greater ease and resilience. For example, when faced with a difficult task, a positive thinker is more likely to approach it with confidence and determination, believing that they can succeed. This mindset not only increases the likelihood of achieving the desired outcome but also reduces the stress and anxiety associated with the task.

Positive thinking also influences how we interact with others. When we maintain an optimistic attitude, we are more likely to be kind, compassionate, and supportive, which can strengthen our relationships and create a more positive social environment. Additionally, positive thinking can enhance our ability to communicate effectively, resolve conflicts, and collaborate with others, leading to more fulfilling and productive interactions.

Furthermore, positive thinking can improve our overall life satisfaction. By focusing on the good in our lives and cultivating a sense of gratitude, we can experience greater happiness and contentment, regardless of external circumstances. This shift in perspective allows us to appreciate the present moment and find joy in the simple pleasures of life.

2.2 Developing a Positive Mindset

While some people may naturally have a more optimistic outlook, positive thinking is a skill that can be developed and strengthened over time. Cultivating a positive mindset involves making a conscious effort to reframe negative thoughts, practice gratitude, and adopt techniques that promote optimism. In this section, we will explore practical strategies for developing a positive mindset, which can lead to lasting changes in how you perceive and respond to life's challenges.

Reframing Negative Thoughts

One of the most effective ways to develop a positive mindset is to reframe negative thoughts. Reframing involves changing the way you interpret and respond to situations, particularly those that trigger negative emotions. By shifting your perspective, you can transform challenges into opportunities for growth and reduce the impact of negative thinking on your well-being.

The first step in reframing negative thoughts is to become aware of them. Many of our negative thoughts are automatic and habitual, making them difficult to recognise. However, by practicing mindfulness and self-reflection, you can start to identify patterns of negative thinking and the underlying beliefs that fuel them.

Once you have identified a negative thought, the next step is to challenge it. Ask yourself whether the thought is based on facts or assumptions and consider alternative explanations or perspectives. For example, if you catch yourself thinking, "I'll never succeed at this," you might challenge that thought by reminding yourself of past successes or considering the possibility that success is achievable with effort and perseverance.

Reframing negative thoughts also involves replacing them with more positive and constructive alternatives. Instead of focusing on what could go wrong, shift your attention to what could go right. For example, if you're feeling anxious about a presentation, instead of thinking, "I'm going to mess up," you might reframe the thought to, "I've prepared well, and I can do this."

Over time, reframing negative thoughts can become a habit, leading to a more positive and optimistic mindset. This shift in thinking can reduce stress, increase resilience, and improve overall well-being.

The Role of Gratitude in Positive Thinking

Gratitude is a powerful tool for cultivating a positive mindset. When we focus on what we are grateful for, we shift our attention away from negative thoughts and experiences, allowing us to appreciate the good in our lives. Practicing gratitude regularly can enhance our sense of well-being, increase life satisfaction, and promote a more positive outlook.

One of the simplest ways to incorporate gratitude into your daily life is to keep a gratitude journal. Each day, take a few minutes to write down three things you are grateful for. These can be small things, like a kind word from a friend, or larger aspects of your life, such as your health or a fulfilling job. By consistently focusing on the positive aspects of your life, you can train your brain to notice and appreciate the good, even during challenging times.

In addition to journaling, you can practice gratitude by expressing appreciation to others. Whether it's thanking someone for their support or acknowledging a kind gesture, expressing gratitude can strengthen relationships and create a positive feedback loop. When you share your gratitude with others, you not only enhance your own well-being but also contribute to a more positive and supportive social environment.

Gratitude can also be practiced in the moment, by taking time to savour positive experiences as they occur. Whether it's enjoying a beautiful sunset, relishing a delicious meal, or appreciating a moment of connection with a loved one, savouring these experiences can deepen your sense of gratitude and enhance your overall happiness.

Techniques to Cultivate Optimism

Optimism is a key component of positive thinking, and it can be cultivated through intentional practice. Optimism involves expecting positive outcomes and believing in your ability to influence your future. While some people may naturally be more optimistic, there are several techniques you can use to develop a more optimistic mindset.

One effective technique is to visualise positive outcomes. Visualisation involves imagining yourself achieving your goals and experiencing success. By vividly picturing these positive scenarios, you can reinforce your belief in your ability to succeed and increase your motivation to take action. Visualisation can be particularly powerful when combined with goal setting, as it helps create a clear and compelling vision of what you want to achieve.

Another technique for cultivating optimism is to practice positive affirmations. Affirmations are positive statements that you repeat to yourself regularly, reinforcing your belief in your abilities and potential. For example, you might say, "I am capable of achieving my goals," or "I choose to focus on the positive." By consistently repeating these affirmations, you can counteract negative self-talk and build a more optimistic mindset.

It's also important to surround yourself with positive influences. The people you spend time with, the content you consume, and the environment you create can all impact your mindset. Seek out relationships, media, and activities that uplift and inspire you, and limit exposure to negativity. By creating a positive environment, you can reinforce your optimism and stay focused on your goals.

Finally, practicing self-compassion is essential for maintaining optimism. Optimism doesn't mean ignoring challenges or setbacks, but rather approaching them with a mindset of growth and resilience. When you encounter difficulties, treat yourself with kindness and understanding, and remind yourself that setbacks are a natural part of the journey. By cultivating self-compassion, you can maintain a positive outlook even in the face of adversity.

2.3 The Benefits of Positive Thinking

The benefits of positive thinking extend far beyond simply feeling good. Positive thinking can have a profound impact on your mental and emotional health, your ability to cope with challenges, and the quality of your relationships. By consistently practicing positive thinking, you can build a foundation for a happier, healthier, and more fulfilling life. In this section, we will explore the various benefits of positive thinking and how they can enhance different areas of your life.

Improving Mental and Emotional Health

Positive thinking is closely linked to improved mental and emotional health. When we focus on the positive aspects of our lives, we reduce stress, anxiety, and depression, and increase feelings of happiness and well-being. Positive thinking can also boost self-esteem and confidence, making it easier to navigate challenges and pursue our goals.

One of the ways positive thinking improves mental health is by reducing the impact of negative emotions. While it's normal to experience negative emotions like sadness, anger, or frustration, dwelling on these emotions can lead to a downward spiral. Positive thinking helps counteract this by shifting our focus to more constructive and empowering thoughts.

Research has shown that positive thinking can also enhance emotional regulation. When we maintain a positive mindset, we are better able to manage our emotions and respond to situations in a balanced and constructive way. This can lead to greater emotional stability and resilience, making it easier to cope with stress and adversity.

Additionally, positive thinking can improve overall life satisfaction. By focusing on the good in our lives and cultivating a sense of gratitude, we can experience greater happiness and fulfillment. This positive outlook can also enhance our sense of purpose and meaning, making it easier to stay motivated and engaged in life.

Building Resilience and Coping Skills

Resilience—the ability to bounce back from adversity—is a key benefit of positive thinking. When we approach challenges with a positive mindset, we are more likely to see them as opportunities for growth, rather than insurmountable obstacles. This shift in perspective can increase our resilience and help us develop more effective coping skills.

Positive thinking encourages a proactive approach to problem-solving. Instead of feeling overwhelmed by difficulties, positive thinkers are more likely to take action and seek solutions. This can lead to greater confidence in their ability to handle challenges, which in turn strengthens resilience.

Moreover, positive thinking can enhance our ability to cope with stress. When we maintain an optimistic outlook, we are less likely to be overwhelmed by stress and more likely to find healthy ways to manage it. This can include practicing relaxation techniques, seeking support from others, or engaging in activities that promote well-being.

Building resilience through positive thinking also involves cultivating a sense of hope and optimism for the future. By focusing on positive outcomes and believing in our ability to achieve them, we can maintain motivation and perseverance, even in the face of setbacks. This forward-looking mindset can help us stay focused on our goals and continue moving forward, no matter what challenges arise.

Enhancing Relationships and Social Interactions

Positive thinking can also have a significant impact on our relationships and social interactions. When we approach others with a positive attitude, we are more likely to build strong, supportive connections and create a positive social environment.

One of the ways positive thinking enhances relationships is by promoting effective communication. Positive thinkers are more likely to express themselves clearly and constructively, which can reduce misunderstandings and conflicts. They are also more likely to listen actively and empathetically, which can strengthen their connections with others.

Positive thinking can also increase our ability to resolve conflicts. When we approach conflicts with a positive mindset, we are more likely to seek solutions that benefit everyone involved, rather than focusing on winning or being right. This can lead to more harmonious and mutually satisfying relationships.

Additionally, positive thinking can increase our capacity for empathy and compassion. When we maintain a positive outlook, we are more likely to see the good in others and respond to their needs with kindness and understanding. This can create a more supportive and nurturing social environment, where everyone feels valued and appreciated.

Finally, positive thinking can enhance our overall social well-being. By focusing on the positive aspects of our relationships and social interactions, we can experience greater satisfaction and fulfillment in our connections with others. This positive outlook can also attract more positive people into our lives, creating a cycle of mutual support and encouragement.

Chapter 3: Overcoming Fear and Anxiety

Fear and anxiety are natural responses to perceived threats, but when they become overwhelming, they can significantly hinder our quality of life. Whether it's fear of failure, anxiety about the future, or irrational phobias, these emotions can hold us back from reaching our full potential. This chapter delves into understanding the roots of fear and anxiety, offers practical techniques for managing these emotions, and explores strategies for overcoming fear. By gaining control over fear and anxiety, you can unlock greater freedom, confidence, and resilience in your life.

3.1 Understanding Fear and Anxiety

Fear and anxiety are emotions that everyone experiences at some point in their lives. They can be triggered by various factors, such as external events, internal thoughts, or past experiences. While fear and anxiety are often used interchangeably, they are distinct emotions with different triggers and effects on our lives. Understanding the psychological roots of fear and anxiety, how they affect us, and the difference between healthy and unhealthy fear is crucial for developing effective strategies to manage and overcome them.

The Psychological Roots of Fear and Anxiety

Fear and anxiety are deeply rooted in our psychology and are essential for survival. From an evolutionary perspective, fear is a protective mechanism that alerts us to danger and prepares us to respond either by fighting, fleeing, or freezing. This response, known as the "fight or flight" reaction, is hardwired into our brains, and has helped humans survive for millennia.

Anxiety on the other hand, is more complex. While fear is typically a response to an immediate threat, anxiety is often triggered by the anticipation of future threats or uncertainties. It is a state of heightened arousal and worry, characterised by a sense of unease or dread. Anxiety can be helpful in small doses, as it can motivate us to prepare for challenges or avoid potential dangers. However, when anxiety becomes chronic or disproportionate to the situation, it can be debilitating.

The psychological roots of fear and anxiety are closely linked to the "amygdala", a part of the brain responsible for processing emotions, particularly those related to danger. When the amygdala detects a threat, it sends signals to the rest of the brain and body to initiate the fight or flight response. While this response is useful in truly dangerous situations, it can be triggered by perceived threats that may not be life-threatening, leading to unnecessary fear and anxiety.

Additionally, fear and anxiety can be influenced by past experiences, particularly those involving trauma. Traumatic events can create lasting imprints on the brain, leading to heightened sensitivity to similar situations in the future. For example, someone who has experienced a car accident may develop a fear of driving, even in safe conditions. Similarly, individuals who have faced significant stress or adversity may be more prone to anxiety, as their brains have become conditioned to expect danger.

How Fear and Anxiety Affect Your Life

Fear and anxiety can have far-reaching effects on your life, influencing your thoughts, emotions, behaviours, and overall well-being. When left unchecked, these emotions can become overwhelming, leading to a range of negative consequences.

One of the most immediate effects of fear and anxiety is the impact on mental and emotional health. Chronic anxiety can lead to persistent worry, restlessness, irritability, and difficulty concentrating. It can also contribute to the development of mental health disorders, such as generalised anxiety disorder, panic disorder, and social anxiety disorder. These conditions can severely limit a person's ability to function in daily life, making it difficult to perform tasks, maintain relationships, or pursue goals.

Fear and anxiety can also affect physical health. The fight or flight response triggers the release of stress hormones, such as adrenaline and cortisol, which can have harmful effects on the body when activated too frequently. Chronic stress from anxiety can lead to a weakened immune system, digestive problems, headaches, and cardiovascular issues. Over time, the cumulative effects of stress can increase the risk of chronic illnesses, such as heart disease and diabetes.

In addition to mental and physical health, fear and anxiety can impact your behaviour and decision-making. When you are driven by fear, you may avoid situations or activities that trigger anxiety, even if they are important for your growth and success. This avoidance can lead to missed opportunities, stalled progress, and a diminished sense of self-efficacy. For example, fear of public speaking may prevent you from pursuing career advancements, or anxiety about failure may keep you from taking on new challenges.

Moreover, fear and anxiety can strain relationships. When you are constantly anxious or fearful, it can be difficult to connect with others or communicate effectively. You may become overly cautious, defensive, or withdrawn, leading to misunderstandings or conflicts with loved ones. In severe cases, fear and anxiety can lead to social isolation, as individuals may withdraw from social interactions to avoid discomfort.

Recognising the impact of fear and anxiety on your life is the first step toward addressing these emotions. By understanding how they manifest and affect your thoughts, behaviours, and well-being, you can begin to develop strategies for managing and overcoming them.

Differentiating Between Healthy and Unhealthy Fear

Not all fear is bad. In fact, healthy fear plays a crucial role in keeping us safe and helping us navigate challenges. The key is to differentiate between healthy and unhealthy fear, so you can respond appropriately to different situations.

Healthy fear is a rational response to a real threat. It prompts you to take action to protect yourself or avoid danger. For example, if you're walking alone at night and notice someone following you, fear may prompt you to take precautions, such as seeking help or finding a safe place. In this case, fear is serving a protective function and helping you stay safe.

Unhealthy fear on the other hand, is disproportionate to the actual threat or is based on irrational beliefs. It may cause you to overestimate the danger or underestimate your ability to cope with it. Unhealthy fear can lead to avoidance behaviours, where you avoid situations that trigger fear, even if they are not truly dangerous. For example, fear of flying may prevent you from traveling, even though flying is statistically one of the safest modes of transportation.

Another sign of unhealthy fear is when it becomes pervasive and interferes with your daily life. If fear is constantly present, preventing you from pursuing your goals, enjoying activities, or maintaining relationships, it has likely crossed the line from healthy to unhealthy. Unhealthy fear can also manifest as phobias—intense, irrational fears of specific objects, situations, or activities that pose little or no actual danger.

The key to managing fear is to recognise when it is healthy and when it is unhealthy. Healthy fear should be acknowledged and acted upon, while unhealthy fear should be challenged and reframed. By learning to differentiate between the two, you can respond to fear in a way that supports your growth and well-being.

3.2 Techniques for Managing Anxiety

Anxiety can be a persistent and overwhelming emotion, but there are effective techniques for managing it. These techniques focus on calming the mind and body, challenging anxious thoughts, and staying grounded in the present moment. By incorporating these strategies into your daily routine, you can reduce the intensity of anxiety and gain greater control over your emotional state.

Breathing Exercises and Relaxation Techniques

One of the most immediate ways to manage anxiety is through breathing exercises and relaxation techniques. These practices help calm the nervous system, reduce the physical symptoms of anxiety, and bring your focus back to the present moment.

Deep Breathing:

Deep breathing is a simple yet powerful technique for reducing anxiety. When you're anxious, your breathing tends to become shallow and rapid, which can exacerbate feelings of panic. Deep breathing on the other hand, involves taking slow, deep breaths that engage the diaphragm. This type of breathing signals the body to relax and can help lower heart rate and blood pressure.

To practice deep breathing, find a quiet place where you can sit or lie down comfortably. Close your eyes and take a deep breath in through your nose, allowing your abdomen to rise as you fill your lungs with air. Hold the breath for a few seconds, then exhale slowly through your mouth, letting all the air out. Repeat this process for several minutes, focusing on the sensation of the breath moving in and out of your body.

Progressive Muscle Relaxation (PMR):

Progressive muscle relaxation is another effective technique for managing anxiety. It involves tensing and then relaxing different muscle groups in the body, helping to release physical tension and promote relaxation.

To practice PMR, start by finding a comfortable position and taking a few deep breaths to relax. Then, begin by tensing the muscles in your feet, holding the tension for a few seconds, and then releasing it. Move up through your body, tensing and relaxing each muscle group in turn, from your legs to your abdomen, chest, arms, and face. As you release the tension, imagine the stress and anxiety leaving your body.

Guided Imagery:

Guided imagery is a relaxation technique that involves visualising a peaceful and calming scene in your mind. This can help distract you from anxious thoughts and create a sense of inner calm.

To practice guided imagery, close your eyes and imagine a place where you feel safe and relaxed. It could be a beach, a forest, a cosy room, or anywhere that brings you comfort. Visualise the details of this place, using all your senses to make the image as vivid as possible. Imagine the sounds, smells, and sensations you would experience if you were there. Spend a few minutes in this mental space, allowing yourself to fully relax and let go of anxiety.

Cognitive Behavioural Techniques for Anxiety:

Cognitive-behavioural therapy (CBT) is a widely used approach for managing anxiety. It focuses on identifying and challenging negative thought patterns that contribute to anxiety and replacing them with more constructive and realistic beliefs.

Cognitive Restructuring:

Cognitive restructuring involves examining and challenging the thoughts that fuel anxiety. Often, anxious thoughts are based on cognitive distortions—irrational or exaggerated beliefs that don't accurately reflect reality. By identifying these distortions, you can reframe your thinking and reduce anxiety.

To practice cognitive restructuring, start by identifying a specific anxious thought. For example, you might think, "I'm going to fail this presentation, and everyone will think I'm incompetent." Next, examine the evidence for and against this thought. Is there concrete evidence that supports this belief, or are you jumping to conclusions? Finally, reframe the thought in a more balanced and realistic way, such as, "I might feel nervous during the presentation, but I've prepared well, and it's okay if I make a few mistakes."

Behavioural Activation:

Behavioural activation is a technique that involves taking action to counteract anxiety and avoidant behaviours. When you're anxious, you may be tempted to avoid situations that trigger anxiety, but this avoidance can reinforce the fear and make it harder to overcome. Behavioural activation encourages you to gradually face your fears and engage in activities that promote well-being.

To practice behavioural activation, start by identifying activities that you avoid due to anxiety. Then, create a plan to gradually expose yourself to these activities in a controlled and manageable way. For example, if you have social anxiety, you might start by attending a small gathering with close friends and gradually work your way up to larger social events. The goal is to build confidence and reduce anxiety through repeated exposure.

Mindfulness-Based CBT:

Mindfulness-based cognitive-behavioural therapy combines traditional CBT techniques with mindfulness practices. Mindfulness involves paying attention to the present moment without judgment, which can help reduce the impact of anxious thoughts.

To practice mindfulness-based CBT, start by bringing your attention to your breath or another focal point, such as the sensations in your body. When anxious thoughts arise, acknowledge them without judgment and gently bring your focus back to the present moment. Over time, this practice can help you become more aware of your thought patterns and reduce the power of anxiety.

Grounding Exercises to Stay Present

Grounding exercises are techniques that help anchor you in the present moment, reducing the intensity of anxiety and preventing you from becoming overwhelmed by anxious thoughts.

5-4-3-2-1 Technique:

The 5-4-3-2-1 technique is a simple grounding exercise that engages your senses to bring your focus back to the present moment. When you're feeling anxious, take a deep breath and follow these steps:

1. Identify five things you can see around you.
2. Identify four things you can touch.
3. Identify three things you can hear.
4. Identify two things you can smell.
5. Identify one thing you can taste.

This exercise helps shift your attention away from anxious thoughts and back to the physical sensations of the present moment.

Body Scan:

A body scan is a mindfulness practice that involves bringing awareness to different parts of your body, helping you stay grounded and connected to the present moment.

To practice a body scan, find a quiet place to sit or lie down comfortably. Close your eyes and take a few deep breaths to relax. Then, slowly bring your attention to different parts of your body, starting with your toes and working your way up to your head. Notice any sensations, tension, or discomfort without judgment, and simply observe them. This practice can help you stay present and reduce the impact of anxious thoughts.

Grounding Statements:

Grounding statements are affirmations or reminders that help you stay focused on the present moment and reduce anxiety. These statements can be repeated silently or aloud when you're feeling anxious.

Examples of grounding statements include:

- "I am safe in this moment."
- "I can handle whatever comes my way."
- "This feeling will pass, and I will be okay."

By repeating these statements, you can reassure yourself and reduce the intensity of anxiety.

3.3 Overcoming Fear

Overcoming fear is a transformative process that requires courage, perseverance, and a willingness to step outside of your comfort zone. While fear can be paralysing, it can also be an opportunity for growth and self-discovery. By facing your fears, building confidence, and embracing uncertainty, you can break free from the limitations that fear imposes on your life.

Facing Your Fears: Exposure Techniques

One of the most effective ways to overcome fear is through exposure techniques. These techniques involve gradually confronting the situations or objects that trigger fear, allowing you to build tolerance and reduce the intensity of the fear response over time.

Gradual Exposure:

Gradual exposure involves breaking down a feared situation into smaller, manageable steps and gradually confronting each step until the fear diminishes. For example, if you have a fear of heights, you might start by standing on a low platform and gradually work your way up to higher levels.

The key to successful gradual exposure is to start with a level of exposure that is challenging but not overwhelming. As you progress through each step, you will build confidence and reduce the fear response, making it easier to confront the next level of exposure.

Systematic Desensitisation:

Systematic desensitisation is a type of exposure therapy that combines gradual exposure with relaxation techniques. The goal is to pair the feared situation with a state of relaxation, reducing the anxiety associated with the fear.

To practice systematic desensitisation, start by creating a hierarchy of feared situations, ranging from least to most anxiety-provoking. Begin with the least feared situation and practice relaxation techniques, such as deep breathing or progressive muscle relaxation, while imagining or confronting the situation. Gradually work your way up the hierarchy, using relaxation techniques to manage anxiety at each step.

Flooding:

Flooding is an exposure technique that involves confronting the feared situation all at once, rather than gradually. This approach can be intense, but it can also lead to rapid reduction of fear. The idea behind flooding is that by fully experiencing the fear without avoiding it, you will eventually realise that the feared outcome does not occur, and the fear will diminish.

Flooding should only be attempted with the guidance of a trained therapist, as it can be overwhelming for some individuals. However, for those who are ready to face their fears head-on, flooding can be a powerful tool for overcoming fear.

Building Courage and Confidence

Courage is not the absence of fear, but the willingness to act in spite of it. Building courage and confidence is essential for overcoming fear and achieving personal growth.

Self-Compassion:

Self-compassion is the practice of treating yourself with kindness and understanding, especially in the face of fear and failure. When you approach fear with self-compassion, you are more likely to take risks and push through challenges, knowing that you will treat yourself with care regardless of the outcome.

To cultivate self-compassion, practice speaking to yourself as you would to a friend. Acknowledge your fears and struggles without judgment and remind yourself that it is okay to feel afraid. By treating yourself with compassion, you can build the courage to face your fears and grow from the experience.

Incremental Success:

One of the best ways to build confidence is through incremental success a small, achievable steps that build on each other over time. When you set and achieve small goals, you reinforce your belief in your ability to succeed, which in turn builds confidence.

To build incremental success, start by setting small, manageable goals that are aligned with your larger objectives. Celebrate each achievement, no matter how small, and use it as motivation to keep moving forward. As you accumulate successes, your confidence will grow, making it easier to tackle bigger challenges.

Visualisation:

Visualisation is a powerful tool for building confidence and overcoming fear. By imagining yourself successfully facing and overcoming your fears, you can create a mental blueprint for success.

To practice visualisation, close your eyes and imagine yourself in a situation that triggers fear. Instead of focusing on the fear, visualise yourself handling the situation with confidence and ease. Imagine the positive outcomes that result from facing your fear and allow yourself to feel the emotions of success. This mental rehearsal can help you build confidence and reduce anxiety when you confront the situation in real life.

Learning to Embrace Uncertainty

Uncertainty is a natural part of life, and learning to embrace it is key to overcoming fear. When we fear the unknown, we often try to control or avoid situations that feel uncertain, which can limit our growth and prevent us from taking risks.

Accepting Uncertainty:

The first step in embracing uncertainty is accepting that it is a normal and inevitable part of life. Instead of trying to eliminate uncertainty, focus on building your tolerance for it. This involves letting go of the need for control and trusting that you can handle whatever comes your way.

Mindfulness:

Mindfulness is a powerful tool for managing uncertainty. By staying present and focusing on the current moment, you can reduce the anxiety that comes from worrying about the future. Mindfulness encourages you to accept uncertainty without judgment, allowing you to move forward with greater ease and confidence.

Reframing Uncertainty as Opportunity:

Another way to embrace uncertainty is by reframing it as an opportunity for growth and discovery. Instead of viewing uncertainty as a threat, see it as a chance to explore new possibilities and learn from new experiences. This shift in perspective can reduce fear and open you up to new opportunities.

Chapter 4: Building Self-Confidence and Self-Esteem

Self-confidence and self-esteem are vital components of a fulfilling and successful life. They shape the way we view ourselves, influence our decisions, and determine how we interact with others. This chapter delves into the nature of self-confidence and self-esteem, exploring their definitions, interrelationship, and the various strategies to enhance them. By strengthening these qualities, you can develop a more positive self-image, overcome challenges with resilience, and lead a life that reflects your true potential.

4.1 Understanding Self-Confidence and Self-Esteem

Self-confidence and self-esteem, though often used interchangeably, are distinct yet interconnected aspects of our psychological makeup. Self-confidence refers to our belief in our abilities to accomplish tasks and face challenges, while self-esteem is the overall sense of self-worth and value, we place on ourselves. Understanding these concepts is the first step toward cultivating a strong foundation of self-assurance and self-respect.

What is Self-Confidence?

Self-confidence is the belief in one's abilities to succeed in various situations. It reflects the trust you have in your skills, judgments, and capacity to achieve goals. Confident individuals approach challenges with a positive outlook, believing that they can handle whatever comes their way.

Self-confidence is not an inherent trait; it is developed over time through experiences and accomplishments. It grows as you build on successes, overcome failures, and learn from your experiences. It's about acknowledging your capabilities and believing that you can navigate life's challenges effectively.

People with high self-confidence tend to take initiative, express their opinions, and are willing to step out of their comfort zones. They are more likely to pursue opportunities, even if there's a risk of failure. Conversely, low self-confidence can lead to self-doubt, hesitation, and missed opportunities. It can also manifest as fear of failure, reluctance to try new things, and a tendency to avoid situations where success is not guaranteed.

Self-confidence is also context specific. You might feel confident in certain areas of your life, such as your career or hobbies, but less so in others, such as social interactions or physical appearance. Building self-confidence involves identifying areas where you lack confidence and working to improve your beliefs and abilities in those areas.

What is Self-Esteem?

Self-esteem is the overall sense of value and respect you have for yourself. It reflects how you view your worth as a person, independent of your achievements or external validation. High self-esteem means you appreciate yourself and believe you are deserving of love, respect, and happiness, regardless of your successes or failures.

Self-esteem is more deeply rooted in your identity than self-confidence. While self-confidence is about what you can do, self-esteem is about who you are. It encompasses your beliefs about your self-worth, your perception of your place in the world, and your acceptance of your strengths and weaknesses.

Healthy self-esteem is characterised by self-acceptance, resilience, and a positive self-image. People with high self-esteem are generally more content with themselves and less affected by external criticism or setbacks. They tend to have healthier relationships, set boundaries, and pursue goals that align with their values.

On the other hand, low self-esteem can lead to self-criticism, insecurity, and a constant need for approval from others. It can result in a negative self-image, where you focus on your flaws and believe you are not worthy of love or success. Low self-esteem can also lead to unhealthy behaviours, such as people-pleasing, avoiding challenges, or engaging in self-sabotage.

Improving self-esteem involves changing the way you view yourself and cultivating a more positive and compassionate relationship with yourself. It requires letting go of negative self-talk, embracing your worth, and recognising that you deserve happiness and success.

The Relationship Between Confidence and Esteem

Self-confidence and self-esteem are closely related, yet they are not the same. Confidence is more about your belief in your abilities, while esteem is about your overall sense of self-worth. However, the two often influence each other. High self-esteem can boost your confidence, as believing in your worth can make you more willing to take on challenges. Similarly, achieving success and building confidence in your abilities can enhance your self-esteem.

For example, if you have high self-esteem, you are likely to approach tasks with a sense of self-assurance, which in turn can lead to successful outcomes and increased confidence. Conversely, if you lack confidence in a specific area, it may negatively affect your self-esteem, making you feel inadequate or unworthy.

Building both self-confidence and self-esteem is crucial for overall well-being. They create a positive feedback loop where confidence fuels self-esteem, and self-esteem reinforces confidence. By understanding the relationship between these two qualities, you can work on developing them in tandem, creating a stronger foundation for personal growth and fulfillment.

4.2 Strategies to Boost Self-Confidence

Boosting self-confidence is a gradual process that involves changing your mindset, recognising your achievements, and embracing your strengths. Confidence is not something you either have or don't have; it's something you can cultivate through deliberate practice and self-awareness. This section explores various strategies, including positive affirmations, visualisation, celebrating small wins, and embracing your strengths, to help you build and maintain self-confidence.

Positive Affirmations and Visualisation

Positive affirmations and visualisation are powerful tools for boosting self-confidence. These techniques involve consciously focusing on positive thoughts and images that reinforce your belief in yourself and your abilities.

Positive Affirmations:

Positive affirmations are statements that you repeat to yourself to challenge and overcome negative thoughts. They are designed to replace self-doubt and negativity with positivity and self-belief. By regularly repeating affirmations, you can rewire your brain to think more positively and build confidence.

To practice positive affirmations, start by identifying areas where you lack confidence. Then, create affirmations that counter those negative beliefs. For example, if you struggle with public speaking, you might repeat affirmations such as, "I am a confident and effective communicator," or "I can handle any situation with calm and poise."

The key to successful affirmations is repetition and consistency. Make it a daily habit to repeat your affirmations, either silently or aloud, and believe in the words you are saying. Over time, these positive statements will become ingrained in your subconscious, helping you build confidence from within.

Visualisation:

Visualisation is another technique that can boost self-confidence by mentally rehearsing successful outcomes. When you visualise, yourself achieving your goals or handling challenging situations with confidence, you create a mental image of success that your mind can draw upon in real life.

To practice visualisation, find a quiet place where you can relax and close your eyes. Imagine yourself in a situation where you want to feel more confident. Picture every detail how you look, how you feel, and how others respond to you. Visualise yourself handling the situation with ease and success. The more vivid and detailed your visualisation, the more effective it will be.

Visualisation works because your brain cannot always distinguish between real and imagined experiences. By visualising success, you can create a sense of familiarity and confidence that translates into real-world situations. Combined with positive affirmations, visualisation can be a powerful tool for building self-confidence.

Celebrating Small Wins

One of the most effective ways to build self-confidence is by celebrating small wins. A small win is any achievement or progress, no matter how minor, that brings you closer to your goals. Recognising and celebrating these wins helps reinforce your belief in your abilities and motivates you to keep moving forward.

Why Small Wins Matter:

Small wins matter because they provide tangible evidence of your progress. When you achieve a small goal, it boosts your confidence and encourages you to tackle bigger challenges. Celebrating small wins also helps break down larger goals into manageable steps, making the overall process less overwhelming.

For example, if you're working on improving your fitness, a small win could be completing your first workout, increasing your reps, or making a healthy meal choice. By celebrating these achievements, you acknowledge your efforts and build momentum for future success.

How to Celebrate Small Wins:

Celebrating small wins doesn't have to be elaborate. It can be as simple as acknowledging your accomplishment, rewarding yourself with a treat, or sharing your success with a friend or loved one. The important thing is to take a moment to recognise your progress and feel proud of your efforts.

To make celebrating small wins a regular practice, consider keeping a journal where you track your achievements. At the end of each day or week, reflect on your progress and write down the small wins you've experienced. This practice not only boosts confidence but also reinforces a positive mindset and a sense of gratitude for your accomplishments.

Embracing Your Strengths and Abilities:

Building self-confidence also involves embracing your strengths and abilities. Everyone has unique talents and qualities that make them special, and recognising and leveraging these strengths can significantly boost your confidence.

Identifying Your Strengths:

To embrace your strengths, you first need to identify them. Take some time to reflect on your skills, talents, and qualities that you excel in. Consider areas where you've received compliments or praise from others, as well as activities that come naturally to you or that you enjoy doing.

You can also seek feedback from friends, family, or colleagues to gain a better understanding of your strengths. Sometimes, others can see strengths in us that we may not recognise ourselves.

Leveraging Your Strengths:

Once you've identified your strengths, find ways to leverage them in your daily life. Focus on tasks and activities that allow you to use your strengths and build confidence. For example, if you're a strong communicator, seek opportunities to lead meetings or give presentations. If you're creative, find outlets for your creativity, such as writing, art, or problem-solving.

Embracing your strengths also means acknowledging and accepting your limitations. No one is good at everything, and that's okay. By focusing on what you excel at, you can build confidence in your abilities and feel more empowered to take on challenges.

Self-Acceptance:

Embracing your strengths also involves self-acceptance. It's about recognising that you are enough just as you are, with all your strengths and weaknesses. Self-acceptance means being kind to yourself, forgiving yourself for mistakes, and appreciating the unique qualities that make you who you are.

When you accept yourself fully, you build a solid foundation of self-confidence that is not easily shaken by external factors. You become more resilient, more authentic, and more capable of achieving your goals.

4.3 Enhancing Self-Esteem

Enhancing self-esteem is a journey of self-discovery and self-acceptance. It involves overcoming self-doubt, practicing self-compassion, and cultivating a positive self-image. By improving your self-esteem, you can develop a deeper sense of self-worth, create healthier relationships, and lead a more fulfilling life.

Overcoming Self-Doubt and Criticism

Self-doubt and self-criticism are common barriers to healthy self-esteem. These negative thought patterns can erode your sense of self-worth and prevent you from reaching your full potential. Overcoming self-doubt and criticism requires challenging these thoughts and replacing them with more positive and constructive beliefs.

Identifying Negative Thought Patterns:

The first step in overcoming self-doubt and criticism is to identify the negative thought patterns that contribute to low self-esteem. These may include thoughts like, "I'm not good enough," "I always mess things up," or "No one likes me." These thoughts are often automatic and ingrained, but they are not necessarily true.

Challenging Negative Thoughts:

Once you've identified your negative thoughts, challenge them by asking yourself whether they are based on facts or assumptions. Are you being too hard on yourself? Are you focusing only on your flaws and ignoring your strengths? By questioning the validity of these thoughts, you can begin to see them for what they are—distorted beliefs that do not reflect reality.

Replacing Negative Thoughts with Positive Ones:

After challenging your negative thoughts, replace them with more positive and realistic ones. For example, if you catch yourself thinking, "I'm not good enough," replace it with, "I am capable and worthy of success." Over time, this practice will help shift your mindset from self-doubt to self-confidence.

Practicing Self-Compassion and Kindness

Self-compassion is the practice of treating yourself with the same kindness and understanding that you would offer to a friend. It involves acknowledging your imperfections and struggles without judgment and offering yourself support and encouragement.

Why Self-Compassion Matters:

Self-compassion is essential for healthy self-esteem because it allows you to accept yourself as you are, without the need for perfection. When you practice self-compassion, you become less critical of yourself and more forgiving of your mistakes. This in turn, helps you build a more positive and resilient self-image.

How to Practice Self-Compassion:

To practice self-compassion, start by noticing when you are being self-critical. When you catch yourself engaging in negative self-talk, pause and ask yourself how you would respond if a friend were in the same situation. Then, offer yourself the same kindness and support that you would offer to a friend.

You can also practice self-compassion through self-care. Take time to nurture your physical, emotional, and mental well-being. Engage in activities that bring you joy, relaxation, and fulfillment. By prioritising your needs and treating yourself with care, you reinforce the belief that you are worthy of love and respect.

Mindful Self-Compassion:

Mindful self-compassion is a practice that combines mindfulness with self-compassion. Mindfulness involves being present in the moment without judgment, while self-compassion involves treating yourself with kindness and understanding.

To practice mindful self-compassion, start by bringing your attention to the present moment. Notice any negative thoughts or emotions that arise and acknowledge them without judgment. Then, offer yourself compassion by saying something like, "It's okay to feel this way," or "I'm doing the best I can." This practice helps you stay connected to your inner self and build a stronger foundation of self-worth.

Cultivating a Healthy Self-Image

A healthy self-image is the cornerstone of self-esteem. It involves seeing yourself in a positive light, embracing your uniqueness, and appreciating your worth. Cultivating a healthy self-image requires changing the way you perceive yourself and developing a more balanced and positive view of who you are.

Body Positivity:

Body positivity is an important aspect of a healthy self-image. It involves accepting and loving your body as it is, regardless of societal standards or external pressures. Body positivity encourages you to focus on what your body can do, rather than how it looks, and to appreciate your physical self for its strengths and capabilities.

To cultivate body positivity, start by challenging negative beliefs about your appearance. Replace self-criticism with self-appreciation. For example, instead of focusing on what you don't like about your body, focus on what you do like and what your body allows you to do. Practice gratitude for your health, strength, and physical abilities.

Self-Reflection:

Self-reflection is a powerful tool for cultivating a healthy self-image. It involves taking time to reflect on your values, strengths, and accomplishments. By regularly engaging in self-reflection, you can gain a deeper understanding of who you are and what makes you unique.

To practice self-reflection, set aside time each day or week to journal or meditate on your thoughts and experiences. Ask yourself questions like, "What are my strengths?" "What am I proud of?" and "What do I value most about myself?" This practice helps you stay connected to your true self and reinforces a positive self-image.

Setting Healthy Boundaries:

Setting healthy boundaries is another key component of a healthy self-image. Boundaries protect your well-being and ensure that your needs and values are respected. When you set boundaries, you reinforce the belief that you are worthy of respect and that your needs matter.

To set healthy boundaries, start by identifying areas in your life where you feel overwhelmed, taken advantage of, or disrespected. Then, communicate your needs and limits clearly and assertively. By standing up for yourself and setting boundaries, you reinforce your self-worth and build a stronger sense of self-esteem.

Chapter 5: Setting and Achieving Goals

Setting and achieving goals is one of the most powerful ways to bring about personal growth and success. Goals give your life direction, motivate you to take action, and provide a sense of purpose and accomplishment. However, the journey from setting goals to achieving them is not always straightforward. This chapter delves into the importance of goal setting, the principles of SMART goals, and the strategies needed to stay committed to your goals. By mastering these concepts, you can create a clear path to success and unlock your full potential.

5.1 The Importance of Goal Setting

Goal setting is not just about making a wish list of things you want to achieve. It is a structured process that requires intention, clarity, and commitment. Goals give your efforts a sense of purpose and direction, turning your dreams into actionable plans. Understanding why goals matter, the psychology behind goal achievement, and the common obstacles you might face can help you approach goal setting with a strategic mindset.

Why Goals Matter

Goals matter because they provide focus, motivation, and a sense of purpose. When you set a goal, you give yourself something to strive for, which helps you stay focused on what's important. Goals act as a roadmap, guiding your decisions and actions toward a desired outcome.

Without clear goals, it's easy to drift through life without a sense of direction. You may find yourself reacting to circumstances rather than proactively shaping your future. Goals help you prioritise your time and energy, ensuring that you are working toward what truly matters to you.

In addition to providing direction, goals also boost motivation. When you have a clear target in mind, you are more likely to stay committed and take the necessary steps to achieve it. Goals give you something to work toward, which can increase your drive and determination.

Goals also foster personal growth. As you work toward your goals, you develop new skills, build resilience, and gain confidence in your abilities. The process of setting and achieving goals helps you grow as a person, both personally and professionally.

The Psychology of Goal Achievement

The psychology of goal achievement is rooted in the idea that setting goals creates a sense of purpose and direction, which in turn motivates you to take action. Psychologically, goals give you something to aim for, which triggers a mental and emotional response that drives behaviour.

One of the key psychological principles behind goal achievement is the concept of "goal-directed behaviour." When you set a goal, your brain becomes focused on achieving that goal, which influences your thoughts, emotions, and actions. This focus creates a sense of urgency and motivation, propelling you toward your desired outcome.

The brain also responds to goals by releasing dopamine, a neurotransmitter associated with pleasure and reward. When you set and achieve goals, your brain releases dopamine, which reinforces positive behaviour and motivates you to continue striving for success.

However, the psychology of goal achievement also involves understanding and managing the challenges that can arise. For example, setting overly ambitious goals can lead to feelings of overwhelm and frustration, while setting vague or unrealistic goals can result in a lack of motivation. To maximise your chances of success, it's important to set clear, achievable goals and break them down into manageable steps.

Common Obstacles to Goal Setting

While setting goals is essential for personal growth and success, it's not without its challenges. Common obstacles to goal setting include fear of failure, procrastination, and a lack of clarity or direction.

Fear of Failure:

Fear of failure is one of the most significant barriers to goal setting. Many people avoid setting goals because they are afraid, they won't be able to achieve them. This fear can lead to self-doubt, hesitation, and a reluctance to take risks. To overcome this obstacle, it's important to shift your mindset and view failure as a learning opportunity rather than a setback.

Procrastination:

Procrastination is another common obstacle to goal setting. Even when you have clear goals in mind, it's easy to put off taking action. Procrastination often stems from a fear of failure, perfectionism, or a lack of motivation. To combat procrastination, break your goals down into smaller, manageable tasks and take action, even if it's just a small step.

Lack of Clarity or Direction:

Setting goals requires clarity and direction. If you're unsure of what you want to achieve or how to get there, it can be challenging to set meaningful goals. To overcome this obstacle, take time to reflect on your values, priorities, and long-term vision. Identify what's most important to you and set goals that align with your aspirations.

5.2 SMART Goals

The SMART goal framework is a powerful tool for setting clear, actionable, and achievable goals. SMART goals are Specific, Measurable, Achievable, Relevant, and Time-Bound. By using this framework, you can create goals that are well-defined and realistic, increasing your chances of success. This section explores the components of SMART goals, the differences between short-term and long-term goals, and how to track your progress and adjust your goals as needed.

Defining SMART Goals: Specific, Measurable, Achievable, Relevant, Time-Bound

SMART goals provide a structured approach to goal setting, ensuring that your goals are clear, actionable, and achievable. Let's break down each component of the SMART framework:

Specific:

A specific goal clearly defines what you want to achieve. It answers the questions of who, what, where, when, and why. A specific goal is focused and unambiguous, making it easier to plan and execute. For example, instead of setting a vague goal like "I want to get fit," a specific goal would be "I want to lose 10 pounds by exercising three times a week and following a healthy diet."

Measurable:

A measurable goal allows you to track your progress and determine when you've achieved your goal. It includes quantifiable criteria that help you assess your success. For example, if your goal is to save money, a measurable goal would be "I want to save $5,000 by the end of the year." This allows you to track your savings and measure your progress over time.

Achievable:

An achievable goal is realistic and attainable given your current resources and constraints. While it's important to challenge yourself, setting a goal that is too ambitious can lead to frustration and discouragement. To ensure your goal is achievable, consider your skills, resources, and the time available to you. For example, if you're new to running, an achievable goal might be "I want to run a 5K in three months" rather than aiming for a marathon right away.

Relevant:

A relevant goal aligns with your values, priorities, and long-term vision. It's a goal that matters to you and is worth pursuing. When setting a goal, ask yourself if it is aligned with your broader life goals and if it will bring you closer to the outcomes you desire. For example, if your long-term goal is to advance your career, a relevant goal might be "I want to complete a professional certification program within the next six months."

Time-Bound:

A time-bound goal has a clear deadline or timeframe for completion. This creates a sense of urgency and motivates you to take action. For example, instead of setting an open-ended goal like "I want to write a book someday," a time-bound goal would be "I want to complete the first draft of my book by December 31." Having a deadline helps you stay focused and accountable.

By applying the SMART framework to your goals, you can create a clear and actionable plan for achieving them. This approach helps you stay organised, motivated, and on track toward success.

Setting Short-Term vs. Long-Term Goals

When setting goals, it's important to distinguish between short-term and long-term goals. Both types of goals play a crucial role in your overall success, but they serve different purposes and require different approaches.

Short-Term Goals:

Short-term goals are objectives that can be achieved in the near future, typically within a few days, weeks, or months. These goals are more immediate and serve as stepping stones toward your long-term aspirations. Short-term goals help you build momentum, stay motivated, and make incremental progress toward your larger goals.

For example, if your long-term goal is to run a marathon, a short-term goal might be to run a 5K within the next three months. Short-term goals are often more specific and actionable, making them easier to achieve.

Long-Term Goals:

Long-term goals are broader objectives that take longer to achieve, typically over several months, years, or even decades. These goals represent your long-term vision and aspirations, such as advancing in your career, achieving financial independence, or mastering a new skill.

While long-term goals provide direction and purpose, they can also be more challenging to achieve due to their complexity and extended timeframes. To stay on track with your long-term goals, it's important to break them down into smaller, more manageable short-term goals.

Balancing Short-Term and Long-Term Goals:

To achieve success, it's essential to balance short-term and long-term goals. Short-term goals keep you focused and motivated in the present, while long-term goals provide a sense of direction and purpose for the future.

When setting goals, start by identifying your long-term aspirations. Then, break them down into smaller, more achievable short-term goals that will help you make progress toward your ultimate objectives. This approach ensures that you stay motivated and on track, while also making steady progress toward your long-term vision.

Tracking Progress and Adjusting Goals

Tracking your progress is a critical component of goal achievement. It allows you to measure your success, stay motivated, and make adjustments as needed. By regularly monitoring your progress, you can ensure that you are on track to achieve your goals and make any necessary changes to your plan.

Why Tracking Progress Matters:

Tracking progress helps you stay accountable and motivated. When you see that you're making progress, it reinforces your commitment to your goals and boosts your confidence. Conversely, if you're not making progress, tracking allows you to identify obstacles and make adjustments to your approach.

Methods for Tracking Progress:

There are several methods you can use to track your progress, depending on the nature of your goals. Some common tracking methods include:

• **Journaling:** Writing down your progress in a journal allows you to reflect on your achievements and challenges. You can track your daily or weekly progress, note any obstacles you encounter, and celebrate your successes.

- **Checklists:** Creating a checklist of tasks or milestones can help you stay organised and focused. As you complete each task, you can check it off the list, providing a visual representation of your progress.

- **Apps and Tools:** There are many apps and tools available that can help you track your progress, such as habit trackers, goal-setting apps, and project management tools. These tools allow you to set reminders, track your achievements, and stay on top of your goals.

Adjusting Goals as Needed:

As you work toward your goals, you may encounter obstacles or changes in circumstances that require you to adjust your goals. It's important to be flexible and adaptable, recognising that your goals may need to evolve over time.

If you find that a goal is no longer relevant or achievable, don't be afraid to revise it. Adjusting your goals doesn't mean giving up, it's a sign of growth and adaptability. By staying open to change and willing to make adjustments, you can ensure that your goals remain aligned with your values and priorities.

5.3 Staying Committed to Your Goals

Staying committed to your goals is essential for achieving success. However, maintaining motivation and focus over the long term can be challenging, especially when faced with distractions, setbacks, and obstacles. This section explores strategies for overcoming procrastination, building accountability systems, and celebrating milestones to stay committed to your goals.

Overcoming Procrastination and Distractions

Procrastination and distractions are common challenges that can derail your progress toward your goals. To stay committed, it's important to develop strategies for overcoming these obstacles and staying focused on your objectives.

Why We Procrastinate:

Procrastination often stems from a fear of failure, perfectionism, or a lack of motivation. When faced with a daunting task or goal, it's easy to put it off in favour of more immediate or enjoyable activities. However, procrastination can prevent you from making progress and achieving your goals.

Strategies for Overcoming Procrastination:

To overcome procrastination, break your goals down into smaller, more manageable tasks. Focus on taking one step at a time, rather than trying to tackle everything at once. Set specific deadlines for each task and hold yourself accountable for completing them.

Another effective strategy is to use the "two-minute rule," which involves starting a task for just two minutes. Once you've started, you're more likely to continue working on the task and make progress.

Managing Distractions:

Distractions can also hinder your progress toward your goals. To stay focused, create a distraction-free environment by eliminating unnecessary interruptions and setting boundaries with others. For example, turn off notifications on your phone, set specific times for checking email, and let others know when you need uninterrupted time to work on your goals.

Building Accountability Systems

Accountability is a powerful tool for staying committed to your goals. When you have someone to hold you accountable, you're more likely to stay on track and follow through on your commitments.

Why Accountability Matters:

Accountability creates a sense of responsibility and commitment. When you share your goals with others, you're more likely to take action and stay motivated. Accountability also provides external support and encouragement, which can help you overcome challenges and stay focused.

Creating Accountability Systems:

There are several ways to build accountability systems, including:

•   **Accountability Partners:** Find a friend, family member, or colleague who shares your goals or is willing to hold you accountable. Check in with each other regularly to share progress, challenges, and successes.

- **Accountability Groups:** Join a group of like-minded individuals who are working toward similar goals. Accountability groups provide a supportive community where you can share your progress, receive feedback, and stay motivated.

- **Coaches or Mentors:** Hiring a coach or mentor can provide professional guidance and accountability. Coaches and mentors can help you set goals, develop strategies, and stay on track.

Self-Accountability:

If you prefer to hold yourself accountable, create a system that works for you. Set specific deadlines, track your progress, and reward yourself for meeting your goals. Self-accountability requires discipline and commitment, but it can be highly effective if you stay focused and motivated.

Celebrating Milestones and Achievements

Celebrating milestones and achievements is an important part of staying committed to your goals. Recognising your progress and rewarding yourself for your accomplishments reinforces positive behaviour and boosts motivation.

Why Celebrating Success Matters:

Celebrating success helps you stay motivated and committed to your goals. When you acknowledge your achievements, you reinforce the belief that your efforts are paying off. Celebrations also provide a sense of satisfaction and fulfillment, which can keep you energised and focused on your next steps.

How to Celebrate Milestones:

Celebrating milestones doesn't have to be elaborate or expensive. It can be as simple as treating yourself to a favourite activity, sharing your success with others, or taking a moment to reflect on your progress.

Consider setting specific milestones for each goal and planning small rewards for reaching them. For example, if your goal is to complete a project, celebrate each phase of the project with a small reward, such as a special meal or a day off.

By celebrating your milestones and achievements, you create positive reinforcement that encourages you to stay committed and continue working toward your goals.

Chapter 6: Developing a Growth Mindset

A growth mindset is the belief that abilities and intelligence can be developed through dedication, effort, and learning. This mindset is foundational for personal development, as it encourages resilience, adaptability, and a love for learning. Developing a growth mindset allows you to see challenges as opportunities, overcome limiting beliefs, and cultivate a positive perspective toward growth and achievement. This chapter will explore the concept of a growth mindset, the techniques to overcome self-limiting beliefs, and how to embrace challenges for personal and professional success.

6.1 The Concept of Growth Mindset

The concept of a growth mindset has gained significant attention in the field of psychology and education, thanks to the work of Dr. Carol Dweck. In her research, Dweck identified two primary mindsets: the fixed mindset and the growth mindset. These mindsets shape how individuals perceive their abilities, approach challenges, and respond to failure. Understanding the differences between these mindsets and how to cultivate a growth-oriented perspective can have a profound impact on your success and well-being.

Understanding Growth vs. Fixed Mindset

A growth mindset is the belief that abilities, intelligence, and talents can be developed through effort, practice, and learning. In contrast, a fixed mindset is the belief that these qualities are innate and unchangeable. People with a fixed mindset often believe that they are born with a certain level of talent or intelligence, and that no amount of effort can change that.

Growth Mindset Characteristics:

•   Embraces challenges as opportunities to learn and grow.

•   Believes that effort leads to improvement and success.

•   Sees failure as a temporary setback and a chance to learn.

•	Values learning and personal development over being "right" or perfect.

•	Is open to feedback and uses it as a tool for improvement.

Fixed Mindset Characteristics:

•	Avoids challenges for fear of failure or appearing incompetent.

•	Believes that effort is pointless if you are not naturally talented or intelligent.

•	Sees failure as a reflection of inherent limitations and a source of shame.

•	Prioritises looking smart or successful over learning and growth.

•	Is defensive about feedback and may see it as a personal attack.

The distinction between these two mindsets is important because it influences how you approach various aspects of life, including education, career, relationships, and personal growth. A growth mindset encourages you to take risks, embrace challenges, and persist in the face of setbacks, all of which are essential for success and fulfillment.

The Impact of Mindset on Success and Failure

Your mindset has a profound impact on your perception of success and failure. With a growth mindset, you view success as a result of effort, learning, and persistence. You understand that setbacks and failures are part of the learning process and that they provide valuable lessons that can lead to future success.

In contrast, a fixed mindset can make you see failure as a reflection of your inherent abilities. You may avoid challenges or give up easily because you believe that effort won't make a difference. This mindset can limit your potential and prevent you from achieving your goals.

Impact on Learning:

In an educational context, students with a growth mindset are more likely to embrace difficult subjects, seek help when needed, and persist through challenges. They see learning as a process and are willing to put in the effort to improve. Conversely, students with a fixed mindset may avoid subjects they find difficult, fear making mistakes, and become discouraged when they encounter challenges.

Impact on Career:

In the workplace, a growth mindset can lead to greater innovation, creativity, and adaptability. Employees with a growth mindset are more likely to take on new challenges, seek feedback, and continuously improve their skills. They are also more resilient in the face of setbacks, which makes them valuable assets to any organisation. On the other hand, a fixed mindset can lead to stagnation, resistance to change, and a fear of failure that hinders professional growth.

Impact on Relationships:

Mindset also affects relationships. People with a growth mindset are more likely to work through conflicts, communicate openly, and view challenges in the relationship as opportunities for growth. They understand that relationships require effort and that both partners can grow and change over time. In contrast, a fixed mindset may lead to a belief that relationships should be easy and that any difficulties are signs of incompatibility.

Cultivating a Growth-Oriented Perspective

Cultivating a growth mindset requires a conscious effort to change your beliefs and behaviours. While it may take time to shift from a fixed mindset to a growth mindset, the benefits are well worth the effort. Here are some strategies to help you cultivate a growth-oriented perspective:

Embrace Challenges:

One of the key aspects of a growth mindset is the willingness to embrace challenges. Instead of avoiding difficult tasks, see them as opportunities to learn and grow. When you encounter a challenge, remind yourself that growth happens outside of your comfort zone. By tackling challenges head-on, you build resilience and confidence in your abilities.

View Failure as a Learning Opportunity:

Failure is an inevitable part of life, but how you respond to it determines your growth. Instead of seeing failure as a reflection of your abilities, view it as a valuable learning experience. Ask yourself, "What can I learn from this?" and "How can I improve next time?" By reframing failure in this way, you turn setbacks into stepping stones for success.

Focus on Effort, Not Just Results:

In a growth mindset, effort is seen as the path to mastery. Instead of focusing solely on the outcome, value the process of learning and improvement. Celebrate your efforts, even if the results aren't perfect. This shift in focus helps you stay motivated and persistent, even when progress is slow.

Seek Feedback:

Feedback is a powerful tool for growth, but it can be difficult to receive, especially if you have a fixed mindset. To cultivate a growth mindset, be open to feedback and view it as a valuable resource for improvement. Instead of taking feedback personally, use it as a guide for your development.

Practice Self-Compassion:

Developing a growth mindset doesn't mean you have to be perfect or always succeed. It's important to be kind to yourself and practice self-compassion. Recognise that growth is a journey, and it's okay to make mistakes along the way. By treating yourself with compassion, you create a supportive environment for learning and growth.

6.2 Overcoming Limiting Beliefs

Limiting beliefs are deeply ingrained thoughts and assumptions that hold you back from reaching your full potential. These beliefs often stem from past experiences, societal conditioning, or self-doubt, and they can create mental barriers that prevent you from pursuing your goals.

Overcoming limiting beliefs is a crucial step in developing a growth mindset, as it allows you to break free from self-imposed limitations and embrace new possibilities. This section explores how to identify self-limiting beliefs, techniques to reframe negative thoughts, and the importance of embracing the process of learning and growth.

Identifying Self-Limiting Beliefs

The first step in overcoming limiting beliefs is to identify them. Limiting beliefs often operate at a subconscious level, shaping your thoughts, behaviours, and decisions without you even realising it. By bringing these beliefs to the surface, you can challenge and replace them with more empowering thoughts.

Common Limiting Beliefs:

- "I'm not good enough."

- "I'll never be successful."

- "I'm too old/young to pursue this goal."

- "I don't deserve happiness."

- "I'm not smart/talented enough."

To identify your limiting beliefs, pay attention to your self-talk and the thoughts that arise when you face challenges or pursue new opportunities. Notice if there are recurring patterns of doubt, fear, or negativity. These thoughts may indicate the presence of a limiting belief.

Journaling Exercise:

One effective way to identify limiting beliefs is through journaling. Take some time to reflect on a goal or challenge you're facing. Write down any negative thoughts or doubts that come to mind. As you review your writing, look for patterns or themes that reveal underlying limiting beliefs.

Question Your Beliefs:

Once you've identified a limiting belief, question its validity. Ask yourself, "Is this belief based on facts or assumptions?" and "What evidence do I have to support or refute this belief?" Challenging your limiting beliefs helps you see them for what they are, mental barriers rather than truths.

Techniques to Reframe Negative Thoughts

Reframing negative thoughts is a powerful technique for overcoming limiting beliefs and developing a growth mindset. By changing the way, you think about a situation, you can shift your perspective and open yourself up to new possibilities.

Cognitive Restructuring:

Cognitive restructuring is a technique used in cognitive-behavioural therapy (CBT) to challenge and change negative thought patterns. The process involves identifying negative thoughts, evaluating their accuracy, and replacing them with more positive and realistic thoughts.

For example, if you have the thought, "I'll never be successful," you can challenge it by asking, "What evidence do I have to support this thought?" and "Are there any times in my life when I have been successful?" By questioning the thought and finding evidence to the contrary, you can replace it with a more empowering belief, such as "I have the ability to achieve success with effort and persistence."

Positive Affirmations:

Positive affirmations are another effective technique for reframing negative thoughts. Affirmations are positive statements that you repeat to yourself to reinforce a positive mindset. By regularly repeating affirmations, you can rewire your brain to focus on positive and empowering beliefs.

For example, if you struggle with self-doubt, you can use affirmations like "I am capable and confident," "I trust in my abilities," or "I am worthy of success." The key to effective affirmations is consistency. Repeat them daily and believe in the truth of the statements.

Visualisation:

Visualisation is a powerful tool for reframing negative thoughts and creating a positive mental image of your goals. When you visualise yourself succeeding, you reinforce the belief that you are capable of achieving your goals. Visualisation can also help reduce anxiety and increase confidence by mentally rehearsing positive outcomes.

To practice visualisation, find a quiet place to sit and close your eyes. Picture yourself achieving your goal in vivid detail. Imagine the sights, sounds, and feelings associated with success. The more detailed and realistic your visualisation, the more powerful it will be in reinforcing a positive mindset.

Embracing the Process of Learning and Growth

Embracing the process of learning and growth is central to developing a growth mindset. This involves shifting your focus from the outcome to the journey and recognising that growth is a continuous process rather than a destination.

The Power of Continuous Learning:

A growth mindset is fuelled by a love of learning and a curiosity for new experiences. When you embrace continuous learning, you open yourself up to new opportunities for growth and development. This mindset encourages you to seek out new knowledge, skills, and experiences, even if they are outside of your comfort zone.

Letting Go of Perfectionism:

Perfectionism can be a major obstacle to growth, as it often leads to fear of failure and avoidance of challenges. To embrace the process of learning, it's important to let go of the need to be perfect and focus instead on progress and improvement. Recognise that mistakes and setbacks are part of the learning process and that they provide valuable lessons for growth.

Celebrate Small Wins:

As you pursue your goals, take time to celebrate small wins along the way. Acknowledging your progress, no matter how small, reinforces a growth mindset and keeps you motivated. Celebrating small wins also helps you stay focused on the journey rather than becoming fixated on the end result.

6.3 Embracing Challenges

Embracing challenges is a fundamental aspect of a growth mindset. Instead of avoiding difficulties or fearing failure, individuals with a growth mindset see challenges as opportunities for learning, growth, and self-improvement. This section explores how to reframe challenges as opportunities, build resilience through adversity, and develop perseverance and tenacity.

Seeing Challenges as Opportunities

Challenges are often seen as obstacles to be avoided or minimised, but with a growth mindset, you can learn to see them as opportunities for growth. When you approach challenges with curiosity and a willingness to learn, you open yourself up to new possibilities and experiences.

Reframing Challenges:

Reframing challenges involves changing your perspective on difficulties. Instead of viewing a challenge as a threat or a potential failure, see it as an opportunity to learn something new, develop a skill, or prove your resilience. Ask yourself, "What can I learn from this challenge?" and "How can I grow as a result of facing this difficulty?"

Embrace Discomfort:

Growth often happens outside of your comfort zone, so it's important to embrace discomfort and uncertainty. When you step out of your comfort zone and take on challenges, you build confidence and resilience. Over time, you become more comfortable with discomfort and more willing to take risks in pursuit of your goals.

The Growth Mindset and Innovation:

Innovation often requires a willingness to take on challenges and explore new ideas. A growth mindset fosters innovation by encouraging you to experiment, take risks, and learn from failure. By embracing challenges and seeing them as opportunities for creative problem-solving, you can drive innovation in your personal and professional life.

Building Resilience Through Adversity

Resilience is the ability to bounce back from setbacks and keep moving forward in the face of adversity. Developing resilience is essential for maintaining a growth mindset, as it allows you to persevere through challenges and setbacks without becoming discouraged.

The Role of Adversity in Growth:

Adversity is often seen as a negative experience, but it can also be a powerful catalyst for growth. When you face and overcome adversity, you develop resilience, confidence, and a deeper understanding of your strengths and capabilities. Adversity can teach you valuable lessons about perseverance, problem-solving, and adaptability.

Building Resilience:

To build resilience, focus on developing a positive and adaptive mindset. Practice self-care, maintain a strong support network, and cultivate a sense of purpose and meaning in your life. Resilience also requires flexibility and the ability to adapt to changing circumstances. By staying open to change and embracing adversity, you strengthen your ability to navigate life's challenges.

The Importance of Support:

Resilience is not something you have to develop on your own. Having a strong support system of friends, family, and mentors can provide you with the encouragement and resources you need to overcome challenges. Don't be afraid to reach out for help when you need it, resilience is often a collective effort.

Developing Perseverance and Tenacity

Perseverance and tenacity are essential qualities for success, especially when facing difficult challenges. With a growth mindset, you understand that persistence and effort are key to overcoming obstacles and achieving your goals.

The Value of Persistence:

Persistence is the ability to keep going, even when progress is slow or setbacks occur. In a growth mindset, persistence is valued because it leads to mastery and success over time. By staying committed to your goals and continuing to put in the effort, you build the skills and resilience needed to overcome challenges.

Cultivating Tenacity:

Tenacity is the determination to keep pushing forward, even in the face of adversity. To cultivate tenacity, focus on your long-term goals and stay motivated by your sense of purpose. Break down challenges into manageable steps, and remind yourself that each step brings you closer to your goal.

The Growth Mindset and Grit:

Grit is a combination of perseverance and passion for long-term goals. A growth mindset fosters grit by encouraging you to stay committed to your goals, even when the going gets tough. By developing grit, you increase your ability to overcome challenges and achieve success in the face of adversity.

Chapter 7: Time Management and Productivity

Time management and productivity are key factors in achieving success in both personal and professional life. Effective time management allows you to prioritise tasks, reduce stress, and make the most of your available time. Productivity on the other hand, focuses on maximising output with the time and resources you have. This chapter will explore the importance of time management, techniques for managing time effectively, and strategies for boosting productivity. By implementing these practices, you can achieve your goals more efficiently and maintain a balanced, stress-free lifestyle.

7.1 The Importance of Time Management

Time is a finite resource, and how you manage it can significantly impact your success and well-being. Time management is more than just organising your schedule; it's about making deliberate choices about how to spend your time to achieve your goals. When you manage your time effectively, you gain control over your life, reduce stress, and increase your productivity. This section will explore why time management is essential, the consequences of poor time management, and the connection between time management and stress.

Why Time Management is Essential for Success

Time management is crucial for success because it helps you allocate your time and resources efficiently to achieve your goals. Whether you're managing a business, pursuing academic goals, or balancing personal responsibilities, effective time management allows you to stay organised, focused, and productive.

Goal Achievement:

When you manage your time effectively, you can prioritise tasks that align with your goals. This ensures that you're making progress toward what matters most, rather than getting bogged down by less important tasks. Time management helps you break down large goals into smaller, manageable steps, making it easier to stay on track and achieve success.

Increased Productivity:

Effective time management enhances productivity by helping you stay focused on tasks and avoid distractions. By organising your time and creating a plan for your day, you can complete tasks more efficiently and reduce wasted time. This increased productivity not only helps you achieve more in less time but also boosts your confidence and motivation.

Work-Life Balance:

Time management also plays a crucial role in maintaining a healthy work-life balance. By organising your time and setting boundaries, you can ensure that you're dedicating time to both work and personal life. This balance is essential for reducing stress, preventing burnout, and maintaining overall well-being.

The Consequences of Poor Time Management

While effective time management can lead to success, poor time management can have significant negative consequences. When you fail to manage your time effectively, you may find yourself overwhelmed, stressed, and unable to achieve your goals.

Missed Deadlines:

One of the most common consequences of poor time management is missed deadlines. When you don't prioritise tasks or allocate sufficient time to complete them, you risk falling behind on important projects. This can lead to a cycle of stress and anxiety, as you scramble to catch up and meet expectations.

Increased Stress and Burnout:

Poor time management can also lead to increased stress and burnout. When you're constantly rushing to complete tasks or feeling overwhelmed by your to-do list, it takes a toll on your mental and physical health. The stress of poor time management can lead to burnout, decreased motivation, and even health problems.

Decreased Productivity:

Ironically, poor time management often results in decreased productivity. When you're disorganised or constantly distracted, it becomes difficult to focus on tasks and complete them efficiently. This lack of productivity can lead to frustration and a sense of being stuck, as you struggle to make progress.

Strained Relationships:

Time management affects not only your work but also your personal life. When you fail to manage your time effectively, you may neglect important relationships with family and friends. This can lead to feelings of guilt, resentment, and strained relationships, as loved ones feel overlooked or undervalued.

The Relationship Between Time Management and Stress

Time management and stress are closely linked. When you manage your time effectively, you reduce stress by creating a sense of control and organisation in your life. On the other hand, poor time management can lead to increased stress and anxiety, as you struggle to keep up with your responsibilities.

The Stress of Overwhelm:

When you have too many tasks and not enough time to complete them, it can lead to a feeling of overwhelm. This stress response triggers the release of cortisol, a hormone that can negatively impact your mood, focus, and overall well-being. Over time, chronic stress from poor time management can lead to burnout and other health issues.

Reducing Stress Through Planning:

Effective time management helps reduce stress by allowing you to plan and organise your tasks. When you have a clear plan for your day and know what needs to be done, it reduces uncertainty and anxiety. By breaking down tasks into manageable steps and setting realistic goals, you can approach your day with confidence and focus.

The Importance of Boundaries:

Setting boundaries is an essential aspect of time management that can also reduce stress. By defining when and how you'll spend your time, you can avoid overcommitting or taking on too much. This helps prevent feelings of overwhelm and ensures that you have time for self-care and relaxation.

7.2 Techniques for Effective Time Management

Effective time management requires more than just making a to-do list. It involves using specific techniques and strategies to prioritise tasks, stay focused, and manage your time efficiently. This section will explore some of the most popular and effective time management techniques, including prioritisation, the Pomodoro Technique, and time blocking. By incorporating these techniques into your daily routine, you can improve your productivity and achieve your goals more efficiently.

Prioritisation: The Eisenhower Matrix

Prioritisation is the process of determining which tasks are most important and should be completed first. The Eisenhower Matrix, also known as the Urgent-Important Matrix, is a powerful tool for prioritisation that helps you categorise tasks based on their urgency and importance.

The Four Quadrants of the Eisenhower Matrix:

•	**Quadrant 1: Urgent and Important:** Tasks that fall into this quadrant require immediate attention and are critical to your goals. Examples include meeting deadlines, handling emergencies, and addressing important issues.

•	**Quadrant 2: Not Urgent but Important:** These tasks are essential for long-term success but don't require immediate action. Examples include planning, goal-setting, and self-care. Focusing on this quadrant can prevent tasks from becoming urgent crises later on.

•	**Quadrant 3: Urgent but Not Important:** Tasks in this quadrant may demand your attention but don't contribute significantly to your goals. Examples include interruptions, meetings, and emails that aren't important. Delegate or minimise these tasks when possible.

•	**Quadrant 4: Not Urgent and Not Important:** These tasks are time-wasters that don't contribute to your success. Examples include excessive social media use, watching TV, or engaging in unproductive activities. Eliminate or limit these tasks to free up time for more important activities.

By categorising tasks into these four quadrants, you can prioritise your time and focus on what truly matters. This technique helps you avoid getting caught up in busy work and ensures that you're making progress toward your goals.

The Pomodoro Technique: Focusing in Short Bursts

The Pomodoro Technique is a time management method that involves breaking your work into short, focused intervals called "Pomodoros," followed by brief breaks. This technique is designed to improve focus and productivity by minimising distractions and preventing burnout.

How the Pomodoro Technique Works:

1. **Choose a Task:** Select a task that you want to work on.

2. **Set a Timer:** Set a timer for 25 minutes (one Pomodoro).

3. **Work on the Task:** Focus exclusively on the task for the entire 25 minutes. Avoid distractions and interruptions during this time.

4. **Take a Short Break:** After the timer goes off, take a 5-minute break. Use this time to stretch, relax, or grab a snack.

5. **Repeat the Process:** After four Pomodoros, take a longer break (15-30 minutes) to recharge.

The Pomodoro Technique is effective because it encourages deep focus and concentration during the work intervals while also allowing time for rest and recovery. By breaking your work into manageable chunks, you can maintain high levels of productivity without feeling overwhelmed or exhausted.

Benefits of the Pomodoro Technique:

•	**Increased Focus:** The short, timed work intervals help you stay focused on the task at hand, reducing the likelihood of distractions.

•	**Reduced Procrastination:** The Pomodoro Technique makes it easier to start tasks, as you only need to commit to 25 minutes of focused work at a time.

•	**Improved Productivity**: The combination of focused work and regular breaks helps prevent burnout and maintain productivity throughout the day.

Time Blocking and Task Scheduling

Time blocking is a time management technique that involves dividing your day into blocks of time, each dedicated to a specific task or activity. This method helps you organise your schedule, prioritise tasks, and ensure that you're making progress toward your goals.

How Time Blocking Works:

1.	**Create a Daily Schedule:** Start by creating a schedule for your day, dividing it into blocks of time (e.g., 30-minute or 1-hour increments).

2.	**Assign Tasks to Each Block:** Assign specific tasks or activities to each time block. Be sure to include time for breaks, meals, and self-care.

3.   Stick to Your Schedule: Follow your time blocks as closely as possible, focusing on the assigned task during each block. Avoid multitasking or switching tasks during a time block.

Time blocking is effective because it forces you to plan your day in advance and commit to specific tasks. This method helps you avoid procrastination, stay organised, and make the most of your time.

Benefits of Time Blocking:

•   **Better Time Allocation:** Time blocking ensures that you're dedicating sufficient time to important tasks, reducing the risk of neglecting key responsibilities.

•   **Increased Focus:** By focusing on one task at a time, you can work more efficiently and reduce distractions.

•   **Improved Work-Life Balance:** Time blocking allows you to allocate time for both work and personal activities, helping you maintain a healthy balance.

7.3 Boosting Productivity

Boosting productivity is about more than just managing your time effectively. It also involves overcoming procrastination, managing your energy levels, and utilising tools and apps to streamline your tasks. This section will explore strategies for overcoming common productivity challenges and provide tips for maximising your output.

Overcoming Procrastination

Procrastination is one of the biggest obstacles to productivity. It occurs when you delay or avoid tasks, often due to fear, perfectionism, or a lack of motivation. Overcoming procrastination requires identifying the underlying causes and implementing strategies to stay focused and motivated.

Identifying the Causes of Procrastination:

• **Fear of Failure:** Many people procrastinate because they fear failing or not meeting expectations. To overcome this fear, focus on the process rather than the outcome and remind yourself that mistakes are part of learning.

• **Perfectionism:** Perfectionists often delay tasks because they want everything to be perfect. To combat this, set realistic expectations and embrace the idea that "done is better than perfect."

• **Lack of Motivation:** When a task feels overwhelming or uninteresting, it's easy to procrastinate. Break the task into smaller, manageable steps and reward yourself for completing each one.

Strategies for Overcoming Procrastination:

• **Set Clear Goals:** Define specific, achievable goals for each task to give yourself a sense of direction and purpose.

- **Use the Two-Minute Rule:** If a task takes less than two minutes to complete, do it immediately. This helps you avoid accumulating small tasks that can become overwhelming.

- **Create a Positive Work Environment**: Minimise distractions and create a workspace that promotes focus and productivity.

Managing Energy, Not Just Time

While time management is important, managing your energy levels is equally crucial for productivity. Your energy fluctuates throughout the day, and understanding when you're most alert and focused can help you maximise your productivity.

Identifying Your Peak Energy Times:

- **Morning:** Many people are most productive in the morning, making it an ideal time for tackling important tasks.

- **Afternoon Slump:** Energy levels often dip in the afternoon, so this may be a good time for less demanding tasks or a break.

- **Evening:** Some people find they have a burst of energy in the evening, which can be used for creative or reflective tasks.

Strategies for Managing Energy:

•   **Take Breaks:** Regular breaks help prevent burnout and maintain energy levels throughout the day. Use techniques like the Pomodoro Technique to structure your breaks.

•   **Stay Hydrated and Nourished**: Dehydration and poor nutrition can lead to fatigue and decreased focus. Stay hydrated and eat balanced meals to maintain your energy levels.

•   **Exercise and Movement:** Physical activity can boost energy and improve focus. Incorporate short walks or stretches into your day to stay energised.

Tools and Apps for Enhanced Productivity

In today's digital age, there are numerous tools and apps designed to enhance productivity and streamline your tasks. These tools can help you stay organised, manage your time, and track your progress.

Popular Productivity Tools and Apps:

•   **Trello:** Trello is a project management tool that allows you to create boards, lists, and cards to organise tasks and projects. It's ideal for visual learners who want to track their progress in a structured way.

•   **Todoist:** Todoist is a task management app that helps you create to-do lists, set deadlines, and prioritise tasks. It's a simple and effective way to stay on top of your responsibilities.

• **RescueTime:** RescueTime is a time-tracking app that monitors your computer and smartphone usage. It provides insights into how you're spending your time and helps you identify areas where you can improve your productivity.

• **Focus@Will:** Focus@Will is a music app designed to improve focus and concentration. It offers a variety of music tracks scientifically proven to enhance productivity.

Maximising the Use of Productivity Tools:

• **Choose the Right Tools:** Select tools that align with your needs and preferences. Experiment with different apps and techniques to find what works best for you.

• **Set Up Notifications and Reminders:** Use notifications and reminders to keep yourself on track and ensure that you don't forget important tasks.

• **Review and Adjust:** Regularly review your productivity tools and systems to ensure they're still effective. Make adjustments as needed to stay organised and productive.

Chapter 8: Mindfulness and Meditation

Mindfulness and meditation have become widely recognised as powerful practices for enhancing mental well-being, reducing stress, and improving overall life satisfaction. These practices, rooted in ancient traditions, have gained modern relevance as people seek ways to cope with the fast-paced demands of everyday life. In this chapter, we will explore what mindfulness is, the benefits it offers for mental and emotional health, various meditation practices, and how to incorporate mindfulness into daily life. By the end of this chapter, you'll have a comprehensive understanding of how mindfulness and meditation can transform your life.

8.1 Understanding Mindfulness

Mindfulness is a practice that involves paying attention to the present moment with an open and non-judgmental attitude. It's about being fully aware of what is happening within and around you, without becoming overly reactive or overwhelmed by your surroundings. Mindfulness can be practiced in various ways, and its benefits extend to all areas of life, from improving mental health to enhancing relationships. In this section, we will explore the concept of mindfulness, its benefits for mental health, and its role in emotional regulation.

What is Mindfulness?

Mindfulness is often defined as the practice of being fully present in the moment, aware of where you are and what you're doing, without being overly reactive or distracted by what's going on around you. At its core, mindfulness is about cultivating a state of awareness where you observe your thoughts, feelings, and sensations without judgment.

The Origins of Mindfulness:

Mindfulness has its roots in Buddhist meditation practices, particularly in the teachings of Vipassana, or insight meditation. However, mindfulness is not exclusive to Buddhism; similar practices can be found in various religious and philosophical traditions, including Hinduism, Taoism, and Stoicism. In recent decades, mindfulness has been secularised and integrated into Western psychology and medicine, where it is used as a tool for stress reduction and mental health.

Key Components of Mindfulness:

• **Awareness:** Mindfulness involves being aware of your thoughts, feelings, bodily sensations, and the environment around you.

• **Non-Judgment:** A crucial aspect of mindfulness is observing without judgment. This means accepting your thoughts and feelings as they are, without labelling them as good or bad.

• **Present Moment:** Mindfulness encourages focusing on the present moment, rather than dwelling on the past or worrying about the future.

The Benefits of Mindfulness for Mental Health

Mindfulness has been extensively studied for its impact on mental health, and research consistently shows that it offers a wide range of benefits. Practicing mindfulness regularly can lead to significant improvements in emotional regulation, stress reduction, and overall mental well-being.

Stress Reduction:

One of the most well-known benefits of mindfulness is its ability to reduce stress. When you practice mindfulness, you learn to focus on the present moment rather than getting caught up in worries about the future or regrets about the past. This shift in focus helps to calm the mind and reduce the physiological effects of stress, such as increased heart rate and blood pressure.

Improved Emotional Regulation:

Mindfulness also enhances emotional regulation by helping you become more aware of your emotions without being overwhelmed by them. By observing your feelings with a non-judgmental attitude, you can create space between your emotions and your reactions. This allows you to respond to situations more thoughtfully rather than reacting impulsively.

Enhanced Focus and Concentration:

Mindfulness can improve focus and concentration by training the mind to stay present. In a world full of distractions, mindfulness helps you maintain attention on the task at hand, leading to greater productivity and efficiency. This can be particularly beneficial in work or academic settings, where sustained attention is crucial.

Reduced Symptoms of Anxiety and Depression:

Studies have shown that mindfulness can significantly reduce symptoms of anxiety and depression. By fostering a non-judgmental awareness of thoughts and feelings, mindfulness helps break the cycle of rumination, a common factor in both anxiety and depression. Mindfulness-based therapies, such as Mindfulness-Based Stress Reduction (MBSR) and Mindfulness-Based Cognitive Therapy (MBCT), have been proven effective in treating these conditions.

The Connection Between Mindfulness and Emotional Regulation

Emotional regulation refers to the ability to manage and respond to emotional experiences in a healthy and balanced way. Mindfulness plays a crucial role in enhancing emotional regulation by increasing self-awareness and helping you observe your emotions without being swept away by them.

Mindfulness and the Brain:

Research has shown that mindfulness can actually change the brain's structure and function. Regular mindfulness practice has been linked to increased activity in the prefrontal cortex, the part of the brain responsible for decision-making and emotional regulation. At the same time, mindfulness reduces activity in the amygdala, the brain's fear centre, which is involved in the stress response.

Creating a Pause:

Mindfulness creates a "pause" between a stimulus and your response, allowing you to choose how to react rather than reacting automatically. This pause is especially helpful in managing intense emotions, such as anger, fear, or sadness. By observing your emotions mindfully, you can respond in a way that aligns with your values and long-term goals, rather than being driven by short-term impulses.

Building Emotional Resilience:

Mindfulness also helps build emotional resilience, which is the ability to bounce back from difficult emotions and challenges. By practicing mindfulness, you become more comfortable with discomfort and uncertainty, which are inevitable parts of life. This resilience allows you to face challenges with a calm and balanced mindset, rather than becoming overwhelmed or discouraged.

8.2 Meditation Practices

Meditation is a practice that involves focusing the mind and eliminating distractions to achieve a state of deep relaxation and awareness. While mindfulness is often considered a form of meditation, there are many different types of meditation practices, each with its own focus and benefits. In this section, we will explore various meditation practices, the difference between guided and solo meditation, and how to integrate meditation into your daily routine.

Different Types of Meditation

Meditation is a broad practice that encompasses many different techniques and approaches. Each type of meditation offers unique benefits, and exploring different methods can help you find the practice that resonates most with you.

- ## **Mindfulness Meditation:**

Mindfulness meditation involves focusing on the present moment and observing your thoughts, feelings, and sensations without judgment. This type of meditation is about cultivating awareness and acceptance of whatever arises in the mind. Mindfulness meditation is often practiced by focusing on the breath, bodily sensations, or sounds.

- ## **Loving-Kindness Meditation (Metta):**

Loving-kindness meditation, or Metta, is a practice that involves cultivating feelings of compassion and love for yourself and others. In this meditation, you repeat phrases such as "May I be happy" or "May you be free from suffering" while focusing on sending positive energy to yourself, loved ones, and even people you may have conflicts with. This practice is particularly effective in fostering empathy, reducing anger, and increasing feelings of connection.

- ## **Body Scan Meditation:**

Body scan meditation is a form of mindfulness meditation that involves paying close attention to different parts of your body, often from head to toe. The goal is to notice any sensations, tension, or discomfort without judgment. This practice helps increase bodily awareness and is often used to reduce stress and promote relaxation.

- ### **Transcendental Meditation:**

Transcendental Meditation (TM) is a technique that involves silently repeating a mantra, a specific word, sound, or phrase during meditation. TM is typically practiced for 20 minutes twice a day and is known for its ability to create a deep state of relaxation and reduce stress.

- ### **Zen Meditation (Zazen):**

Zen meditation, or Zazen, is a form of seated meditation that is central to Zen Buddhism. In this practice, you sit in a specific posture and focus on your breath or a koan (a paradoxical question or statement). The goal of Zen meditation is to cultivate a state of alertness and presence, often leading to insights into the nature of existence.

- ### **Guided Visualisation:**

Guided visualisation is a meditation practice that involves following a guided narrative to imagine a peaceful and relaxing scene or situation. This type of meditation is often used for stress reduction, relaxation, and goal setting. By visualising positive outcomes, you can influence your mindset and behaviour in real life.

Guided Meditation vs. Solo Practice

Meditation can be practiced with guidance (guided meditation) or independently (solo practice). Both approaches have their own benefits, and the choice between them depends on your personal preferences and experience level.

Guided Meditation:

In guided meditation, an instructor or audio recording leads you through the meditation process. This can be especially helpful for beginners who are new to meditation and may find it challenging to focus or know what to do. Guided meditation provides structure and direction, making it easier to stay on track and achieve a deep state of relaxation.

Benefits of Guided Meditation:

•   **Structure:** Guided meditation provides a clear framework for the practice, making it easier to follow along and stay focused.

•   **Accessibility:** Many guided meditations are available online or through apps, making it easy to find a practice that suits your needs.

•   **Variety:** Guided meditations can cover a wide range of topics, from stress reduction to sleep improvement, allowing you to tailor your practice to your specific goals.

Solo Practice:

Solo meditation, or unguided meditation, involves meditating independently without external guidance. This approach allows for greater flexibility and personalisation of your practice. Solo meditation is often preferred by experienced practitioners who are comfortable with the meditation process and want to explore their practice more deeply.

Benefits of Solo Meditation:

•   **Flexibility:** Solo meditation allows you to meditate at your own pace and in your own way, without following a set script or structure.

•   **Deeper Exploration:** Without external guidance, solo meditation encourages you to explore your own mind and experiences more deeply.

•   **Self-Reliance:** Solo meditation fosters self-reliance and independence, as you learn to guide yourself through the practice.

Integrating Meditation into Your Daily Routine

One of the keys to reaping the benefits of meditation is to practice it regularly. Integrating meditation into your daily routine doesn't have to be time-consuming or complicated. Even a few minutes of meditation each day can make a significant difference in your mental and emotional well-being.

Tips for Establishing a Daily Meditation Practice:

•   **Start Small:** If you're new to meditation, start with just 5-10 minutes a day. As you become more comfortable with the practice, you can gradually increase the duration.

•   **Choose a Time:** Find a time of day that works best for you, whether it's in the morning, during a lunch break, or before bed. Consistency is key, so try to meditate at the same time each day.

- **Create a Meditation Space:** Designate a quiet, comfortable space in your home where you can meditate without distractions. This space should be free from noise and clutter, allowing you to focus fully on your practice.

- **Use Apps or Tools:** If you prefer guided meditation, use apps like Headspace, Calm, or Insight Timer to access a variety of guided sessions. These apps can also help you track your progress and stay motivated.

- **Be Patient:** Meditation is a skill that takes time to develop. Don't get discouraged if your mind wanders or if you find it challenging at first. With regular practice, meditation will become easier and more enjoyable.

8.3 Living Mindfully

Mindfulness is not just something you practice during meditation; it's a way of living that can be applied to every aspect of your life. Living mindfully means bringing awareness and presence to your daily activities, whether you're eating, walking, or simply breathing. By cultivating mindfulness in your everyday life, you can reduce stress, enhance your well-being, and experience a greater sense of fulfillment. In this section, we will explore how to live mindfully through practices like mindful eating, walking, and breathing, and how mindfulness can help reduce stress and anxiety.

Mindful Eating, Walking, and Breathing

Mindfulness can be integrated into simple, everyday activities such as eating, walking, and breathing. These practices help you stay connected to the present moment and cultivate a deeper appreciation for the small things in life.

Mindful Eating:

Mindful eating involves paying full attention to the experience of eating, from the taste and texture of the food to the sensations in your body. This practice encourages you to slow down, savour each bite, and listen to your body's hunger and fullness cues. Mindful eating can help you develop a healthier relationship with food, reduce overeating, and enhance your enjoyment of meals.

Steps for Mindful Eating:

•	**Eat Slowly:** Take your time with each bite, chewing slowly and savouring the flavours and textures.

•	**Engage Your Senses:** Notice the colours, smells, and tastes of your food. Pay attention to the sensations in your mouth and the feeling of fullness in your stomach.

•	**Avoid Distractions:** Turn off the TV, put away your phone, and focus solely on the act of eating. This allows you to fully experience your meal without distractions.

Mindful Walking:

Mindful walking is a practice that involves paying attention to the sensations of walking, such as the movement of your legs, the feeling of your feet on the ground, and the rhythm of your breath. This practice can be done anywhere, whether you're walking in nature or through a busy city. Mindful walking helps you stay grounded and connected to the present moment, while also providing the physical benefits of movement.

Steps for Mindful Walking:

• **Focus on Your Steps:** Pay attention to each step, feeling the ground beneath your feet and the movement of your body.

• **Sync with Your Breath:** Coordinate your steps with your breath, taking a few steps for each inhale and exhale.

• **Observe Your Surroundings:** Notice the sights, sounds, and smells around you without getting lost in thought. Simply observe and appreciate the environment.

Mindful Breathing:

Mindful breathing is a simple yet powerful practice that involves focusing on your breath and observing it without trying to change it. This practice can be done anywhere and at any time, making it an accessible tool for reducing stress and bringing your attention back to the present moment.

Steps for Mindful Breathing:

•   **Focus on Your Breath:** Bring your attention to your breath, noticing the sensation of the air entering and leaving your nostrils or the rise and fall of your chest.

•   **Observe Without Judgment:** Simply observe your breath as it is, without trying to change its rhythm or depth. If your mind wanders, gently bring your focus back to your breath.

•   **Practice Regularly:** Incorporate mindful breathing into your daily routine, whether it's for a few minutes in the morning, during a break, or before bed.

Cultivating Presence in Daily Activities

Living mindfully means bringing presence and awareness to all of your daily activities, no matter how mundane or routine they may seem. By practicing mindfulness in everyday tasks, you can transform ordinary moments into opportunities for relaxation, reflection, and joy.

Mindfulness in Daily Tasks:

•   **Washing Dishes:** Rather than rushing through chores, try washing dishes mindfully. Focus on the sensation of the warm water, the texture of the soap, and the sound of the running tap.

•   **Brushing Your Teeth:** Pay attention to the feeling of the toothbrush against your teeth and gums, the taste of the toothpaste, and the movement of your hand.

- **Driving:** Instead of getting lost in thought or becoming frustrated in traffic, practice mindful driving. Notice the sensation of your hands on the steering wheel, the movement of the car, and the scenery passing by.

Benefits of Mindfulness in Daily Activities:

- **Reduced Stress:** By staying present and focused, you can reduce the stress that comes from worrying about the future or dwelling on the past.

- **Increased Enjoyment:** Mindfulness allows you to fully engage in and appreciate even the simplest activities, leading to greater life satisfaction.

- **Enhanced Relationships:** Mindfulness can improve your relationships by helping you listen more attentively, communicate more effectively, and respond with greater empathy and understanding.

Using Mindfulness to Reduce Stress and Anxiety

Mindfulness is a powerful tool for reducing stress and anxiety, both of which are common challenges in today's fast-paced world. By practicing mindfulness, you can calm your mind, reduce the physiological effects of stress, and develop a more balanced and resilient response to life's challenges.

How Mindfulness Reduces Stress:

Mindfulness helps reduce stress by encouraging a focus on the present moment, which can alleviate the constant stream of worries that often fuel stress and anxiety. By observing your thoughts and feelings without judgment, mindfulness helps you create distance from negative thinking patterns and prevents you from getting caught up in them.

Mindfulness for Anxiety:

Anxiety often arises from a fear of the unknown or a focus on worst-case scenarios. Mindfulness helps counteract anxiety by grounding you in the present moment and allowing you to observe your anxious thoughts without becoming overwhelmed by them. Over time, this practice can reduce the intensity and frequency of anxious feelings.

Practical Mindfulness Techniques for Stress Reduction:

• **Body Scan Meditation:** Use body scan meditation to release tension and relax your body, which in turn calms your mind.

• **Mindful Breathing:** Practice mindful breathing to bring your focus back to the present moment whenever you feel stressed or anxious.

• **Mindful Movement:** Engage in mindful movement, such as yoga or tai chi, to connect with your body and release physical and mental stress.

Chapter 9: Finding Purpose and Meaning in Life

Purpose and meaning are the driving forces that give our lives direction and fulfillment. They are the reasons we wake up in the morning, the motivations behind our actions, and the guiding lights in both good times and bad. While some people naturally find purpose early in life, others may spend years searching for it. Regardless of where you are on your journey, discovering your purpose and integrating it into your life can lead to greater happiness, resilience, and overall well-being. In this chapter, we will explore the importance of purpose, techniques for discovering it, and ways to live a meaningful life that aligns with your values and goals.

9.1 The Importance of Purpose

Purpose is often described as the reason for which something is done or created, or for which something exists. In the context of human life, purpose is the sense of meaning and direction that gives our lives coherence and significance. Without purpose, life can feel aimless, directionless, and devoid of fulfillment. Understanding the importance of purpose and how it influences our lives is the first step toward living a life that feels meaningful and satisfying.

Understanding the Role of Purpose in Life Satisfaction

Purpose plays a critical role in life satisfaction, which is the degree to which individuals feel content with their lives. Research consistently shows that people who have a clear sense of purpose tend to experience higher levels of life satisfaction, better mental health, and a greater sense of well-being. When you have a sense of purpose, you are more likely to feel that your life has meaning, that your efforts are worthwhile, and that you are contributing to something larger than yourself.

The Psychological Benefits of Purpose:

•   **Increased Happiness:** Having a sense of purpose is strongly correlated with higher levels of happiness. Purpose gives you a reason to engage with life, pursue goals, and invest in relationships, all of which contribute to overall happiness.

- **Reduced Risk of Depression:** Purpose acts as a buffer against depression. When you have a clear sense of what you want to achieve and why it matters, you are less likely to succumb to feelings of hopelessness or despair.

- **Greater Life Satisfaction:** Purposeful living leads to greater life satisfaction by providing a sense of accomplishment and meaning. You are more likely to feel that your life is on the right track and that you are making progress toward your goals.

Purpose as a Source of Meaning:

Meaning is the deep sense of fulfillment that comes from knowing that your life matters and that your actions are making a positive impact. Purpose is the primary source of meaning in life. Whether your purpose is to raise a family, contribute to your community, advance in your career, or pursue a creative passion, having a purpose provides a sense of direction and significance.

How Purpose Influences Motivation and Resilience

Purpose is a powerful motivator. When you have a clear sense of purpose, you are more likely to set goals, take action, and persist in the face of challenges. Purpose gives you a reason to push through obstacles, stay committed to your goals, and keep moving forward, even when the going gets tough.

Purpose as a Driver of Motivation:

Motivation is the force that drives you to take action and pursue your goals. Purpose fuels motivation by giving you a clear reason for why you are doing what you are doing. When you understand the "why" behind your actions, you are more likely to stay focused, disciplined, and determined.

Resilience and Purpose:

Resilience is the ability to bounce back from setbacks and challenges. Purpose enhances resilience by providing a sense of direction and meaning during difficult times. When you have a strong sense of purpose, you are better equipped to handle adversity, as you can see your challenges in the context of your larger goals. Purpose gives you the strength to persevere, even when things seem overwhelming.

Purpose and Long-Term Goals:

Purpose also influences the types of goals you set and how you approach them. People with a strong sense of purpose tend to set long-term goals that align with their values and beliefs. These goals provide a sense of direction and help you stay focused on what truly matters, even when faced with short-term distractions or challenges.

Exploring Your Personal Values and Beliefs

Discovering your purpose often begins with exploring your personal values and beliefs. Values are the principles and standards that guide your behaviour, while beliefs are the convictions you hold about what is true and important. By identifying your values and beliefs, you can gain clarity on what matters most to you and what you want to achieve in life.

Identifying Core Values:

Your core values are the fundamental beliefs that shape your decisions, actions, and interactions with others. These values influence everything from how you spend your time to how you treat others and how you define success.

Questions to Explore Your Values:

•	What are the most important principles that guide your life?

•	What qualities do you admire in others?

•	What are the non-negotiables in your life, for example things you are unwilling to compromise on?

•	What activities or pursuits make you feel most fulfilled?

Aligning Values with Purpose:

Once you have identified your core values, the next step is to align them with your sense of purpose. Purpose-driven goals should reflect your values and be consistent with what you believe is important. For example, if one of your core values is compassion, your purpose might involve helping others or making a positive impact on your community.

Exploring Beliefs and Mindsets:

In addition to values, your beliefs and mindsets also play a key role in shaping your sense of purpose. These beliefs include your views about yourself, others, and the world around you. Positive and empowering beliefs can support your sense of purpose, while limiting beliefs may hold you back from living a purposeful life.

Challenging Limiting Beliefs:

To discover your purpose, it may be necessary to challenge and reframe limiting beliefs. For example, if you believe that you are not capable of achieving your goals or that your efforts won't make a difference, these beliefs can undermine your sense of purpose. By adopting a growth mindset and embracing the belief that you can learn, grow, and make a positive impact, you can unlock new possibilities for purposeful living.

9.2 Discovering Your Purpose

Discovering your purpose is a deeply personal journey that requires introspection, self-awareness, and exploration. While some people may have a clear sense of purpose from a young age, others may need time and reflection to uncover what truly drives them. In this section, we will explore techniques for finding your life's purpose, aligning your actions with your purpose, and overcoming obstacles that may stand in the way of living a purposeful life.

Techniques for Finding Your Life's Purpose

Finding your purpose often involves asking deep questions, reflecting on your experiences, and exploring your passions and interests. The following techniques can help guide you on this journey of self-discovery.

Reflect on Your Passions and Interests:

One of the most effective ways to discover your purpose is to reflect on what you are passionate about. What activities, causes, or pursuits make you feel excited and fulfilled? Your passions often hold clues to your purpose, as they reflect what you truly care about and what gives you energy.

Questions to Explore Your Passions:

•   What activities do you lose track of time while doing?

•   What topics or issues do you feel strongly about?

•   What hobbies or interests bring you joy and satisfaction?

Consider Your Strengths and Talents:

Your strengths and talents are the unique abilities and skills that you bring to the world. These strengths can also provide insight into your purpose, as they represent areas where you have the potential to make a significant impact.

Questions to Explore Your Strengths:

•   What are you naturally good at?

•   What do others often praise you for or seek your help with?

•   What tasks or challenges do you find easy or enjoyable to tackle?

Reflect on Meaningful Experiences:

Another way to discover your purpose is to reflect on past experiences that have been particularly meaningful or impactful. These experiences often provide valuable insights into what matters most to you and what you want to achieve in life.

Questions to Explore Meaningful Experiences:

•   What moments in your life have brought you the greatest sense of fulfillment?

•   What challenges have you faced that have shaped your values and beliefs?

• What accomplishments or contributions are you most proud of?

Explore Your Legacy:

Thinking about the legacy you want to leave behind can also help you discover your purpose. What do you want to be remembered for? What impact do you want to have on others and the world?

Questions to Explore Your Legacy:

• How do you want to be remembered by your family, friends, and community?

• What contributions do you want to make to society or the world?

• What lasting impact do you want to leave behind?

Connect with Others:

Sometimes, discovering your purpose involves seeking guidance and inspiration from others. Connecting with mentors, role models, or supportive communities can provide valuable insights and help you clarify your purpose.

Questions to Explore Through Connection:

• Who are the people you admire, and what is it about their lives that inspires you?

• How can you learn from others who are living purposeful lives?

- What role can community and relationships play in helping you discover and live your purpose?

Aligning Your Actions with Your Purpose

Once you have a clearer sense of your purpose, the next step is to align your actions with it. Living a purposeful life requires more than just understanding your purpose, it involves actively pursuing it through your choices, goals, and daily activities.

Set Purpose-Driven Goals:

Purpose-driven goals are goals that reflect your values and align with your sense of purpose. These goals provide a clear path forward and help you stay focused on what truly matters.

Steps for Setting Purpose-Driven Goals:

- **Identify Your Purpose:** Clearly articulate your purpose and the values that guide it.

- **Set Specific Goals:** Define specific, actionable goals that align with your purpose.

- **Break Down Goals:** Break your larger goals into smaller, manageable steps that you can work on each day.

- **Stay Flexible:** Be open to adjusting your goals as your purpose evolves and new opportunities arise.

Prioritise Purposeful Actions:

In addition to setting goals, it is important to prioritise actions that reflect your purpose. This may involve making choices that align with your values, even when they are challenging or inconvenient.

Steps for Prioritising Purposeful Actions:

•   **Evaluate Your Choices:** Regularly assess whether your actions are aligned with your purpose.

•   **Make Purpose-Driven Decisions:** When faced with decisions, consider how each option aligns with your purpose and values.

•   **Stay Committed:** Stay committed to your purpose, even when it requires sacrifice or persistence.

Integrate Purpose into Daily Life:

Living a purposeful life is not just about pursuing big goals; it is also about finding meaning in everyday activities. By integrating purpose into your daily life, you can experience greater fulfillment and joy in the present moment.

Steps for Integrating Purpose into Daily Life:

•   **Practice Mindfulness:** Stay present and mindful in your daily activities, finding meaning in even the simplest tasks.

•   **Reflect Daily:** Take time each day to reflect on how your actions align with your purpose.

- **Celebrate Small Wins:** Recognise and celebrate the small steps you take toward living your purpose.

Overcoming Obstacles to Living Purposefully

Living a purposeful life is not always easy. There are often obstacles and challenges that can make it difficult to stay true to your purpose. However, by recognising and addressing these obstacles, you can continue to move forward on your path.

Overcoming Fear and Doubt:

Fear and self-doubt are common obstacles to living purposefully. These feelings can prevent you from taking risks, pursuing your goals, or staying committed to your purpose.

Steps for Overcoming Fear and Doubt:

- **Acknowledge Your Fears:** Recognise and acknowledge the fears and doubts that are holding you back.

- **Challenge Limiting Beliefs:** Reframe negative thoughts and beliefs that undermine your sense of purpose.

- **Take Action:** Take small, courageous steps toward your purpose, even in the face of fear.

Navigating Life Transitions:

Life transitions, such as career changes, family responsibilities, or personal loss, can create uncertainty and disrupt your sense of purpose. During these times, it's important to stay connected to your values and continue pursuing what matters most.

Steps for Navigating Life Transitions:

•	**Stay Grounded in Your Values:** Stay connected to your core values and beliefs, even when circumstances change.

•	**Adapt Your Purpose:** Be open to evolving your purpose as your life changes and new opportunities arise.

•	**Seek Support:** Reach out to supportive communities or mentors who can help you navigate transitions.

Balancing Purpose with Practicalities:

Living a purposeful life sometimes involves balancing your purpose with practical responsibilities, such as work, finances, or family obligations. While this can be challenging, it's possible to find ways to integrate purpose into your daily life.

Steps for Balancing Purpose with Practicalities:

•	**Set Realistic Expectations:** Recognise that living purposefully doesn't mean neglecting your practical responsibilities.

•	**Find Synergy:** Look for ways to align your purpose with your work, relationships, and daily activities.

•	**Prioritise Self-Care:** Take care of your physical and mental well-being so that you have the energy and resilience to pursue your purpose.

9.3 Living a Meaningful Life

Living a meaningful life means more than just discovering your purpose, it involves integrating that purpose into your daily actions, inspiring others, and sustaining a sense of meaning over time. In this section, we will explore how to live mindfully and purposefully, how to inspire others through your actions, and how to maintain a sense of meaning throughout your life's journey.

Integrating Purpose into Your Daily Life

Integrating purpose into your daily life involves finding ways to live in alignment with your values and goals on a consistent basis. This means making purposeful choices, staying mindful of your actions, and continually reflecting on how you can live more authentically.

Steps for Integrating Purpose into Daily Life:

•	**Set Daily Intentions:** Start each day by setting intentions that align with your purpose. Consider what actions you can take to move closer to your goals and live in alignment with your values.

- **Stay Present:** Practice mindfulness throughout your day, staying present and engaged in your activities. This helps you stay connected to your purpose and find meaning in even the smallest tasks.

- **Reflect and Adjust:** Regularly reflect on your actions and consider whether they are aligned with your purpose. Be open to making adjustments and staying flexible as you continue to grow and evolve.

Purposeful Living and Fulfillment:

By integrating purpose into your daily life, you can experience greater fulfillment and satisfaction. Living purposefully means that your actions are guided by your values, and you are continuously working toward something that is meaningful and important to you.

Inspiring Others Through Purposeful Living

One of the most powerful aspects of living a purposeful life is the ability to inspire others. When you live in alignment with your values and pursue your goals with passion and determination, you naturally become a source of inspiration and motivation for those around you.

Ways to Inspire Others:

- **Lead by Example:** Show others what is possible by living your purpose with integrity and commitment. Your actions can serve as a model for how to live a meaningful and purposeful life.

- **Share Your Story:** Share your journey of discovering and living your purpose with others. By being open and honest about your experiences, you can inspire others to explore their own sense of purpose.

- **Encourage and Support:** Encourage others to pursue their passions and live in alignment with their values. Offer support, guidance, and encouragement as they embark on their own journey of purposeful living.

The Ripple Effect of Purposeful Living:

When you live purposefully, your actions create a ripple effect that extends beyond your own life. By inspiring others to live with purpose, you contribute to a larger movement of positive change and meaningful impact.

Sustaining a Sense of Meaning Over Time

Living a meaningful life is an ongoing process that requires continuous reflection, growth, and adaptation. As you move through different stages of life, your sense of purpose may evolve, and you may encounter new challenges and opportunities. Sustaining a sense of meaning over time involves staying connected to your values, embracing change, and remaining open to new possibilities.

Strategies for Sustaining Meaning:

- **Regular Reflection:** Take time to regularly reflect on your purpose and how it aligns with your current life circumstances. This reflection helps you stay connected to what matters most and allows you to make necessary adjustments.

- **Embrace Change:** Recognise that your purpose may evolve as you grow and change. Be open to new experiences, challenges, and opportunities that can deepen your sense of meaning.

- **Cultivate Gratitude:** Practice gratitude for the journey you are on and the progress you have made. Gratitude helps you stay grounded and appreciative of the meaningful moments in your life.

Finding Meaning in Every Season:

Life is full of different seasons, each with its own challenges and opportunities. By staying connected to your purpose and remaining open to growth and change, you can find meaning in every season of life.

The Legacy of Purposeful Living:

Ultimately, living a purposeful and meaningful life is about leaving a positive legacy. Your actions, contributions, and impact will continue to resonate long after you are gone. By living with purpose, you create a lasting legacy that inspires others and contributes to the greater good.

Chapter 10: Managing Stress and Burnout

In our fast-paced, demanding world, stress and burnout have become common experiences for many people. While stress is a natural response to challenging situations, chronic stress can lead to burnout—a state of emotional, physical, and mental exhaustion caused by prolonged stress. Understanding how to manage stress and prevent burnout is essential for maintaining overall well-being and achieving a balanced, fulfilling life. This chapter will explore the difference between stress and burnout, techniques for managing stress, and strategies for preventing and recovering from burnout.

10.1 Understanding Stress and Burnout

Stress is a natural part of life. It is the body's response to any demand or challenge that disrupts our sense of balance. While stress can be a motivator and help us meet deadlines or navigate difficult situations, chronic stress can have detrimental effects on our physical and mental health. When stress becomes overwhelming and unrelenting, it can lead to burnout, a state of exhaustion that goes beyond typical stress. In this section, we will explore the difference between stress and burnout, how chronic stress affects your health, and how to recognise the signs of burnout.

The Difference Between Stress and Burnout

While stress and burnout are related, they are not the same. Understanding the difference between the two can help you recognise when you are experiencing typical stress versus when you are at risk of burnout.

What is Stress?

Stress is the body's natural response to challenges or demands. It can be triggered by various factors, such as work pressure, personal responsibilities, financial concerns, or major life changes. Stress can be both positive (eustress) and negative (distress). Eustress is the type of stress that motivates you to take action, meet deadlines, and perform well under pressure. Distress, on the other hand, occurs when stress becomes overwhelming and negatively impacts your well-being.

Common Symptoms of Stress:

• **Physical:** Headaches, muscle tension, fatigue, sleep disturbances, digestive issues.

• **Emotional:** Anxiety, irritability, mood swings, feelings of overwhelm.

• **Behavioural**: Procrastination, changes in appetite, difficulty concentrating, social withdrawal.

What is Burnout?

Burnout is a state of emotional, physical, and mental exhaustion caused by prolonged stress. Unlike stress, which can come and go, burnout is a chronic condition that develops over time when stress is not effectively managed. Burnout often results from a combination of excessive demands, lack of support, and a sense of helplessness or hopelessness.

Common Symptoms of Burnout:

• **Emotional Exhaustion:** Feeling drained, overwhelmed, and unable to cope.

• **Depersonalisation:** A sense of detachment from work, relationships, or daily activities.

• **Reduced Performance**: A decline in productivity, creativity, and motivation.

Key Differences Between Stress and Burnout:

•	**Stress:** Involves feeling overwhelmed but still able to function; may include periods of high energy and motivation.

•	**Burnout:** Involves feeling completely drained and unable to function; characterised by emotional numbness and a sense of hopelessness.

The Progression from Stress to Burnout:

Burnout often develops gradually as stress accumulates over time. Initially, you may feel stressed but still able to cope. However, as stress becomes chronic and unrelenting, it can lead to physical and emotional exhaustion, ultimately resulting in burnout.

How Chronic Stress Affects Your Health

Chronic stress has a profound impact on both physical and mental health. While the body is equipped to handle short bursts of stress, prolonged exposure to stress can lead to a range of health issues.

Physical Health Effects of Chronic Stress:

•	**Cardiovascular Issues**: Chronic stress increases the risk of heart disease, high blood pressure, and stroke. Stress triggers the release of stress hormones like cortisol and adrenaline, which can lead to inflammation, increased heart rate, and elevated blood pressure.

- **Immune System Suppression:** Stress weakens the immune system, making you more susceptible to infections, illnesses, and chronic conditions. This can result in frequent colds, flu, or other infections.

- **Digestive Problems:** Stress can disrupt the digestive system, leading to issues such as irritable bowel syndrome (IBS), acid reflux, and stomach ulcers. Chronic stress can also affect appetite and digestion, leading to weight gain or loss.

- **Muscle Tension and Pain:** Stress causes muscles to tense up, leading to headaches, neck and back pain, and other musculoskeletal issues.

- **Sleep Disturbances:** Chronic stress often results in difficulty falling asleep, staying asleep, or experiencing restful sleep. Poor sleep further exacerbates stress and can lead to a cycle of exhaustion and irritability.

Mental Health Effects of Chronic Stress:

- **Anxiety and Depression:** Chronic stress is a significant risk factor for developing anxiety disorders and depression. Persistent stress can lead to feelings of helplessness, hopelessness, and a sense of being overwhelmed.

- **Cognitive Impairment:** Stress can impair cognitive functions such as memory, concentration, and decision-making. Chronic stress can also lead to "brain fog," making it difficult to think clearly and stay focused.

- **Emotional Dysregulation:** Chronic stress can lead to mood swings, irritability, and difficulty managing emotions. This can strain relationships and negatively impact overall well-being.

Stress and the Brain:

Chronic stress affects the brain's structure and function. The hippocampus, which is responsible for memory and learning, can shrink under prolonged stress. The prefrontal cortex, which is involved in decision-making and emotional regulation, can also be negatively impacted. This can lead to difficulties in problem-solving, impulse control, and emotional stability.

The Importance of Addressing Chronic Stress:

Given the wide-ranging effects of chronic stress on health, it is essential to address stress proactively. Ignoring stress or simply "pushing through" can lead to burnout and long-term health issues. Developing effective stress management techniques is crucial for maintaining overall well-being and preventing burnout.

Recognising the Signs of Burnout

Recognising the signs of burnout is critical for addressing it before it becomes debilitating. Burnout often manifests gradually, and many people may not realise they are experiencing it until it has significantly impacted their lives.

Emotional Signs of Burnout:

• **Emotional Exhaustion:** Feeling completely drained and emotionally depleted, even after rest. You may feel like you have nothing left to give.

• **Detachment and Isolation:** Feeling disconnected from work, relationships, or daily activities. You may withdraw from social interactions and lose interest in things you once enjoyed.

• **Cynicism and Pessimism:** Developing a negative or cynical outlook on life, work, or the future. You may feel that nothing you do makes a difference and lose motivation to try.

Physical Signs of Burnout:

• **Chronic Fatigue:** Feeling physically exhausted, even after a full night's sleep. You may struggle to get out of bed or find the energy to complete daily tasks.

• **Sleep Disturbances:** Difficulty falling asleep, staying asleep, or experiencing restful sleep. You may wake up feeling tired and unrefreshed.

• **Physical Symptoms:** Experiencing headaches, muscle tension, gastrointestinal issues, or other unexplained physical symptoms.

Behavioural Signs of Burnout:

• **Decreased Performance:** A decline in productivity, creativity, and motivation. You may find it difficult to concentrate, complete tasks, or meet deadlines.

• **Procrastination**: Avoiding tasks or responsibilities due to a lack of energy or motivation. You may feel overwhelmed by even simple tasks.

• **Increased Irritability:** Becoming easily frustrated, angry, or impatient with others. You may have difficulty managing your emotions and react more strongly to stressors.

When to Seek Help:

If you recognise the signs of burnout in yourself, it is essential to take action. Burnout is not something that will resolve on its own and ignoring it can lead to more severe health issues. Seeking support from a mental health professional, counsellor, or coach can help you develop strategies for recovery and prevent burnout from recurring.

10.2 Techniques for Stress Management

Effective stress management is essential for preventing burnout and maintaining overall well-being. While stress is an inevitable part of life, there are various techniques and practices that can help you manage stress and reduce its impact on your health. In this section, we will explore stress-relief practices such as exercise, meditation, and relaxation; time management and boundary setting; and the role of sleep and nutrition in stress management.

Stress-Relief Practices: Exercise, Meditation, and Relaxation

Incorporating stress-relief practices into your daily routine can help you manage stress more effectively and prevent it from becoming overwhelming. Exercise, meditation, and relaxation techniques are some of the most effective ways to reduce stress and promote mental and physical well-being.

Exercise:

Physical activity is one of the most effective ways to reduce stress. Exercise helps release endorphins, the body's natural mood enhancers, and reduces the levels of stress hormones such as cortisol. Regular exercise can also improve sleep, boost energy levels, and enhance overall well-being.

Types of Exercise for Stress Relief:

• **Aerobic Exercise:** Activities such as running, swimming, cycling, or dancing can help reduce stress and improve cardiovascular health.

• **Strength Training:** Weightlifting, resistance exercises, or bodyweight exercises can help build physical strength and reduce tension.

• **Yoga and Stretching:** Yoga and stretching exercises promote relaxation, flexibility, and mindfulness, making them excellent for stress relief.

How to Incorporate Exercise into Your Routine:

•   **Start Small:** If you're new to exercise, start with short, manageable workouts and gradually increase the duration and intensity.

•   **Find Activities You Enjoy:** Choose exercises that you find enjoyable and fulfilling to increase your motivation and consistency.

•   **Make It a Habit:** Schedule regular exercise sessions into your daily routine and treat them as non-negotiable appointments.

Meditation:

Meditation is a powerful tool for managing stress and promoting relaxation. It involves focusing your attention on the present moment and cultivating a sense of calm and awareness. Regular meditation practice can help reduce anxiety, improve emotional regulation, and enhance overall mental clarity.

Types of Meditation for Stress Relief:

•   **Mindfulness Meditation:** Focuses on being present and aware of your thoughts, feelings, and sensations without judgment. This practice helps you stay grounded and reduce stress.

•   **Breath Awareness Meditation:** Involves focusing on your breath as a way to calm the mind and body. Deep, intentional breathing can help reduce stress and promote relaxation.

- **Loving-Kindness Meditation:** Focuses on cultivating compassion and kindness toward yourself and others. This practice can help reduce negative emotions and promote emotional well-being.

How to Incorporate Meditation into Your Routine:

- **Start with Short Sessions:** Begin with just a few minutes of meditation each day and gradually increase the duration as you become more comfortable.

- **Find a Quiet Space:** Choose a quiet, comfortable space where you can meditate without distractions.

- **Be Consistent:** Try to meditate at the same time each day to establish a consistent practice.

Relaxation Techniques:

Relaxation techniques such as deep breathing, progressive muscle relaxation, and visualisation can help reduce stress and promote a sense of calm.

Types of Relaxation Techniques:

- **Deep Breathing:** Involves taking slow, deep breaths to calm the nervous system and reduce stress. This technique can be done anywhere, anytime you feel stressed.

- **Progressive Muscle Relaxation:** Involves tensing and then relaxing different muscle groups in the body to release tension and promote relaxation.

- **Visualisation:** Involves imagining a peaceful, calming scene or experience to reduce stress and promote a sense of well-being.

How to Incorporate Relaxation Techniques into Your Routine:

- **Practice Daily:** Set aside time each day to practice relaxation techniques, even if it's just for a few minutes.

- **Combine with Other Activities:** Incorporate relaxation techniques into your daily activities, such as deep breathing during a commute or visualisation before bed.

Time Management and Boundary Setting

Effective time management and setting clear boundaries are essential for managing stress and preventing burnout. By organising your time and protecting your personal space, you can reduce the pressure and demands that contribute to stress.

1. Prioritise Tasks:

One of the most effective ways to manage stress is to prioritise your tasks and focus on what's most important. This involves identifying your most critical tasks and completing them first, while delegating or postponing less important tasks.

Steps for Prioritising Tasks:

- **Create a To-Do List:** Write down all your tasks and responsibilities and organise them by priority.

- **Use the Eisenhower Matrix:** The Eisenhower Matrix is a tool that helps you categorise tasks into four quadrants: urgent and important, important but not urgent, urgent but not important, and neither urgent nor important. Focus on the tasks that are both urgent and important first.

- **Avoid Multitasking:** Focus on one task at a time to increase productivity and reduce stress.

2. Set Boundaries:

Setting boundaries is essential for protecting your time and energy. This involves saying no to unnecessary demands, setting limits on work hours, and protecting your personal time.

Steps for Setting Boundaries:

- **Communicate Clearly:** Clearly communicate your boundaries to others, whether it's setting limits on work hours, saying no to additional responsibilities, or protecting your personal time.

- **Protect Your Time:** Schedule regular breaks, downtime, and self-care activities into your daily routine. Treat these activities as non-negotiable.

- **Practice Saying No:** Learn to say no to requests or demands that don't align with your priorities or values. Saying no is a powerful way to protect your time and energy.

Avoid Overcommitment:

Overcommitting to too many tasks or responsibilities can lead to overwhelm and stress. It's essential to be realistic about what you can handle and avoid taking on more than you can manage.

Steps for Avoiding Overcommitment:

•	**Assess Your Capacity:** Before agreeing to new tasks or responsibilities, assess your current workload and capacity.

•	**Delegate When Possible:** If you're feeling overwhelmed, delegate tasks to others or ask for help.

•	**Be Honest with Yourself:** Be honest with yourself about what you can realistically handle. It's better to do a few tasks well than to spread yourself too thin.

The Role of Sleep and Nutrition in Stress Management

Sleep and nutrition play a critical role in managing stress and maintaining overall well-being. Poor sleep and unhealthy eating habits can exacerbate stress and make it more difficult to cope with life's demands.

The Importance of Sleep:

Sleep is essential for physical and mental recovery. During sleep, the body repairs itself, consolidates memories, and regulates emotions. Chronic sleep deprivation can lead to increased stress, irritability, and difficulty concentrating.

Tips for Improving Sleep:

• **Establish a Sleep Routine:** Go to bed and wake up at the same time each day, even on weekends.

• **Create a Relaxing Bedtime Ritual:** Develop a bedtime ritual that helps you unwind and prepare for sleep, such as reading, meditating, or taking a warm bath.

• **Limit Screen Time Before Bed:** Avoid using electronic devices at least an hour before bed, as the blue light from screens can interfere with sleep.

The Role of Nutrition:

Nutrition plays a significant role in managing stress and supporting overall health. A balanced diet can help regulate mood, energy levels, and stress hormones.

Tips for a Stress-Reducing Diet:

• **Eat a Balanced Diet:** Include a variety of whole foods, such as fruits, vegetables, whole grains, lean proteins, and healthy fats, in your diet.

• **Stay Hydrated:** Drink plenty of water throughout the day to stay hydrated and support overall health.

• **Limit Caffeine and Sugar:** While caffeine and sugar can provide a temporary energy boost, they can also lead to energy crashes and increased stress.

Mindful Eating:

Practicing mindful eating can help reduce stress and improve your relationship with food. This involves paying attention to the taste, texture, and sensations of food, as well as being aware of hunger and fullness cues.

Tips for Mindful Eating:

•   **Eat Slowly:** Take your time to chew and savour each bite of food.

•   **Avoid Distractions:** Focus on your meal without distractions, such as watching TV or scrolling on your phone.

•   **Listen to Your Body:** Pay attention to hunger and fullness cues, and eat until you are satisfied, not overly full.

10.3 Preventing and Recovering from Burnout

Burnout is a serious condition that can have long-lasting effects on your physical and mental health. Preventing burnout involves proactive strategies to manage stress, set boundaries, and maintain a healthy work-life balance. If you are already experiencing burnout, recovery requires taking time to rest, re-evaluate your priorities, and make changes to your lifestyle. In this section, we will explore strategies for preventing burnout, recovery techniques for burnout, and building a sustainable work-life balance.

Strategies for Preventing Burnout

Preventing burnout requires a proactive approach to managing stress and maintaining a healthy balance between work and personal life. By implementing the following strategies, you can reduce the risk of burnout and protect your overall well-being.

1. Prioritise Self-Care:

Taking care of yourself is essential for preventing burnout. This includes regular exercise, proper nutrition, sufficient sleep, and time for relaxation and hobbies.

Tips for Prioritising Self-Care:

•	**Schedule Regular Breaks:** Take regular breaks throughout the day to rest and recharge, whether it's a short walk, stretching, or simply stepping away from your desk.

•	**Practice Mindfulness:** Incorporate mindfulness practices into your daily routine to stay present and reduce stress.

•	**Engage in Hobbies:** Make time for hobbies and activities that bring you joy and relaxation, whether it's reading, painting, gardening, or playing a musical instrument.

2. Set Realistic Expectations:

Setting realistic expectations for yourself and others can help prevent burnout. This involves being honest about what you can realistically accomplish and avoiding overcommitting.

Tips for Setting Realistic Expectations:

• **Assess Your Capacity:** Regularly assess your workload and responsibilities to ensure that you are not taking on too much.

• **Communicate Clearly:** Communicate your limits and expectations to others, whether it's at work or in your personal life.

• **Be Kind to Yourself:** Avoid perfectionism and be kind to yourself when things don't go as planned. It's okay to adjust your expectations as needed.

3. Build a Support System:

Having a strong support system can help prevent burnout by providing emotional support, encouragement, and practical assistance. Surround yourself with people who understand and support your goals and well-being.

Tips for Building a Support System:

• **Connect with Loved Ones:** Maintain regular connections with family and friends who provide emotional support and a sense of community.

- **Seek Professional Support:** Consider seeking support from a therapist, counsellor, or coach to help you navigate challenges and prevent burnout.

- **Join Supportive Communities:** Join groups or communities that share your interests or goals, whether it's a hobby group, professional network, or online community.

Recovery Techniques for Burnout

If you are already experiencing burnout, it's essential to take steps to recover and restore your well-being. Recovery from burnout involves rest, self-reflection, and making changes to your lifestyle and work habits.

Take a Break:

The first step in recovering from burnout is to take a break from the source of stress. This may involve taking time off work, reducing your workload, or stepping back from responsibilities.

Tips for Taking a Break:

- **Request Time Off:** If possible, take time off work to rest and recover. Use this time to focus on self-care and relaxation.

- **Set Boundaries:** Reduce your workload by delegating tasks or saying no to additional responsibilities. Prioritise your well-being over productivity.

- **Disconnect:** Consider disconnecting from work-related communication during your break to give yourself a mental and emotional break.

Reflect and Re-evaluate:

During your break, take time to reflect on the factors that contributed to your burnout and re-evaluate your priorities and goals.

Tips for Reflection and Re-evaluation:

- **Identify Stressors:** Reflect on the specific stressors that contributed to your burnout, whether it's work demands, lack of support, or personal pressures.

- **Re-evaluate Priorities:** Consider what is most important to you and how you can align your actions with your values and goals.

- **Make Changes:** Based on your reflections, make changes to your lifestyle, work habits, or boundaries to prevent burnout from recurring.

Focus on Recovery:

Recovery from burnout requires focusing on rest, self-care, and rebuilding your energy and motivation.

Tips for Focusing on Recovery:

- **Rest and Recharge:** Prioritise rest and relaxation during your recovery period. Focus on activities that bring you joy and relaxation.

•	**Rebuild Your Energy:** Gradually rebuild your energy through regular exercise, proper nutrition, and sufficient sleep.

•	**Seek Support:** Don't hesitate to seek support from loved ones, therapists, or coaches during your recovery. Having a strong support system can help you navigate the challenges of recovery.

Building a Sustainable Work-Life Balance

A sustainable work-life balance is essential for preventing burnout and maintaining overall well-being. By creating a balance between work and personal life, you can reduce stress, increase satisfaction, and protect your health.

Set Clear Boundaries:

Setting clear boundaries between work and personal life is essential for maintaining a healthy balance. This involves defining when work ends, and personal time begins.

Tips for Setting Boundaries:

•	**Define Work Hours:** Establish clear work hours and stick to them. Avoid working late or bringing work home unless absolutely necessary.

•	**Protect Personal Time: Prioritise** personal time for relaxation, hobbies, and spending time with loved ones. Treat personal time as non-negotiable.

•	**Disconnect After Work:** Consider disconnecting from work-related communication after work hours to protect your personal time.

Prioritise What Matters:

Focusing on what matters most to you can help you create a balance between work and personal life that aligns with your values and goals.

Tips for Prioritising What Matters:

•	**Identify Priorities:** Reflect on what is most important to you, whether it's your career, family, health, or personal growth.

•	**Align Actions with Priorities:** Make decisions and take actions that align with your priorities and values.

•	**Let Go of Non-Essentials**: Be willing to let go of tasks or responsibilities that don't align with your priorities or add unnecessary stress.

Practice Self-Compassion:

Practicing self-compassion is essential for maintaining a healthy work-life balance. This involves being kind to yourself, recognising your limits, and avoiding perfectionism.

Tips for Practicing Self-Compassion:

•	**Be Kind to Yourself:** Treat yourself with the same kindness and understanding that you would offer to a friend.

•	**Recognise Your Limits:** Acknowledge your limits and avoid pushing yourself beyond them. It's okay to take breaks and ask for help when needed.

- **Celebrate Small Wins:** Celebrate your achievements, no matter how small, and recognise the effort you put into maintaining a healthy balance.

Chapter 11: Cultivating Resilience and Grit

Resilience and grit are two of the most powerful attributes one can develop to navigate life's challenges. Resilience refers to the ability to bounce back from adversity, while grit is the perseverance and passion to achieve long-term goals despite obstacles. These qualities are not just traits you're born with, but skills that can be cultivated and strengthened over time. Developing resilience and grit is essential for overcoming setbacks, pursuing your goals, and ultimately achieving success.

In this chapter, we will explore the importance of resilience and grit, provide practical strategies for building these traits, and share real-life examples of individuals who have demonstrated exceptional resilience and grit in their lives.

11.1 Understanding Resilience and Grit

Resilience and grit may seem like similar concepts, but they serve different purposes in the journey toward personal growth and success. Resilience is about how you recover from adversity, while grit is the determination to pursue long-term goals even when faced with difficulties. Both qualities are essential for navigating life's inevitable ups and downs.

In this section, we'll explore the importance of resilience in overcoming adversity, the role of grit in achieving success, and how emotional intelligence plays a crucial role in building resilience.

The Importance of Resilience in Overcoming Adversity

Resilience is the psychological strength that helps you recover from setbacks and challenges, whether it be personal, professional, or emotional challenges. It is the mental toughness that allows you to bounce back after these challenges and continue pursuing your goals. Resilience is not just about surviving difficult times; it's about thriving despite them. It involves adaptability, flexibility, and a positive mindset that focuses on learning from experiences rather than being defeated by them.

Key Aspects of Resilience:

• **Adaptability:** Life is full of unexpected twists and turns. Resilient individuals are flexible and able to adapt to new circumstances, making them more capable of managing stress and uncertainty. For example, during the COVID-19 pandemic, many people had to adapt to remote work, home schooling, and other changes to their daily lives. Those who were resilient found ways to adjust and cope with these challenges.

• **Optimism:** Maintaining a positive outlook, even in tough situations, is a hallmark of resilience. Optimistic people are more likely to see challenges as temporary and surmountable, which helps them stay motivated and focused on finding solutions. Studies have shown that optimism can lead to better health outcomes and increased life satisfaction.

• **Support Systems:** Having strong relationships and a supportive network can bolster resilience by providing emotional and practical help during difficult times. Whether it's friends, family, or colleagues, having people to lean on can make all the difference when you're facing adversity.

Real-Life Examples of Resilience:

• **Nelson Mandela:** After spending 27 years in prison, Mandela emerged as a symbol of resilience, leading South Africa out of apartheid and becoming its first Black president. His ability to forgive and move forward, despite the injustices he faced, exemplifies the power of resilience.

- **J.K. Rowling:** Before her success with the Harry Potter series, Rowling faced numerous rejections and personal struggles, including living as a single mother on welfare. Yet her resilience enabled her to keep writing and ultimately achieve worldwide success.

- **Malala Yousafzai:** Malala's resilience was evident when she continued to advocate for girls education even after being targeted by the Taliban. Her courage and determination to recover and continue her mission despite the physical and emotional trauma exemplify deep resilience.

What is Grit? How Persistence Leads to Success

Grit, as defined by psychologist Angela Duckworth, is the combination of passion and perseverance toward long-term goals. It's the ability to maintain focus and effort over extended periods, even when progress is slow, or obstacles arise. Grit is often more predictive of success than talent or intelligence because it reflects a deep commitment to one's goals.

Unlike resilience, which is about bouncing back, grit is about pushing forward. It's the relentless pursuit of your objectives, despite setbacks or failures. Gritty individuals are those who wake up every day determined to make progress, over extended periods, no matter how small it is, which is essential for achieving significant accomplishments.

Key Components of Grit:

1.   Passion for Learning: Cultivating a passion for continuous learning can enhance your grit. By staying curious and committed to expanding your knowledge, you maintain motivation and perseverance. For instance, a scientist who remains dedicated to their research despite numerous setbacks shows grit through their passion for discovery.

2.   Goal Alignment: Aligning your goals with your values and interests helps sustain your motivation over time. When your goals resonate deeply with you, you're more likely to persevere. For example, an entrepreneur who is passionate about sustainable business practices will likely show greater perseverance in developing eco-friendly products.

3.   Long-Term Vision: Developing a clear long-term vision helps you maintain focus and determination. Break your vision into actionable steps and regularly revisit it to stay motivated. For example, an athlete who envisions winning an Olympic medal will set incremental goals and stay committed to their training regimen.

Real-Life Examples of Grit in Achieving Success:

•   **Angela Duckworth's Research:** Angela Duckworth, a psychologist who popularised the concept of grit, found that grit is a more reliable predictor of success than IQ. Her research on West Point cadets showed that those with higher levels of grit were more likely to complete the rigorous training program.

- **Thomas Edison:** Known for his persistence, Edison made thousands of unsuccessful attempts before inventing the lightbulb. His famous quote, "I have not failed. I've just found 10,000 ways that won't work," exemplifies the grit needed to achieve ground-breaking success.

- **Michael Jordan:** Despite being cut from his high school basketball team, Jordan's grit and relentless work ethic led him to become one of the greatest basketball players of all time. His determination to improve and succeed, even in the face of failure, is a testament to the power of grit.

The Role of Emotional Intelligence in Resilience

Emotional intelligence (EI) is the ability to recognise, understand and manage your own emotions, as well as the emotions of others. It plays a crucial role in developing resilience because it helps you navigate the emotional challenges that come with adversity. High EI allows you to remain composed under pressure, empathise with others, and maintain positive relationships even during difficult situations.

How Emotional Intelligence Enhances Resilience:

- **Self-Awareness:** Being aware of one's emotions enables individuals to recognise when they are feeling stressed or overwhelmed, allowing them to take proactive steps to manage their emotions. For example, if you notice that you're feeling anxious before a big presentation, you can use self-awareness to identify the root cause of your anxiety and address it.

- **Self-Regulation:** The ability to control and manage emotions, especially in stressful situations, is essential for resilience. Self-regulation helps individuals remain calm and focused, even in the face of adversity. Techniques like deep breathing, mindfulness, and cognitive reframing can help with self-regulation.

- **Empathy:** Understanding and empathising with others emotions can strengthen relationships and provide emotional support during tough times. Empathy allows you to connect with others on a deeper level and offer comfort and encouragement when they need it most. For example, empathising with a colleague's struggles can help you offer meaningful support and strengthen your professional relationship.

- **Social Skills:** Effective communication and conflict resolution skills can help individuals navigate challenges in relationships, which in turn enhances their resilience. Building strong social connections is a key aspect of emotional intelligence and resilience.

Real-Life Example:

- **J.K. Rowling**: Rowling's perseverance in the face of rejections from multiple publishers demonstrates the role of grit in achieving success. Her passion for storytelling and commitment to her craft eventually led to the global success of the Harry Potter series.

- **Barack Obama:** Throughout his presidency, Obama demonstrated high emotional intelligence, particularly in his ability to remain calm under pressure, empathise with others, and navigate complex social dynamics. His resilience in the face of criticism and challenges was bolstered by his emotional intelligence.

11.2 Building Resilience

Resilience is not an inherent trait but a skill that can be developed and strengthened over time. Building resilience involves cultivating emotional strength, learning from setbacks, and adopting strategies that promote mental well-being. In this section, we'll explore techniques for bouncing back from setbacks, developing emotional strength, and learning from failures and mistakes.

Techniques for Bouncing Back from Setbacks

Setbacks are an inevitable part of life, but how we respond to them can make all the difference. Resilience involves the ability to recover quickly from disappointments and keep moving forward.

Strategies for Bouncing Back:

- **Reframe the Situation:** Instead of viewing a setback as a failure, see it as an opportunity to learn and grow. Reframing challenges in a positive light can help shift your mindset and reduce the emotional impact of the setback. For example, if you didn't get a job you applied for, you could reframe the situation by recognising that it wasn't the right fit and that another opportunity will come along.

- **Focus on Solutions:** When faced with a setback, focus on finding solutions rather than dwelling on the problem. Taking proactive steps to address the issue can help you regain control and move forward. This might involve seeking advice, brainstorming alternative approaches, or simply taking a break to gain perspective.

- **Practice Self-Compassion:** Be kind to yourself during difficult times. Recognise that setbacks are a normal part of life and avoid harsh self-criticism. Self-compassion can help you maintain emotional balance and resilience, making it easier to recover from setbacks.

- **Physical Activity:** Regular physical activity is a proven stress reliever that can boost your resilience. Exercise releases endorphins, which are natural mood lifters, and can help you feel more capable of handling challenges.

- **Social Support:** Building a strong support network is essential for resilience. Surround yourself with people who encourage and uplift you, and don't hesitate to reach out for help when needed.

Real-Life Example:

- **Steve Jobs:** After being ousted from Apple, the company he co-founded, Jobs demonstrated resilience by starting new ventures, including Pixar, and eventually returning to lead Apple to unprecedented success. His ability to bounce back from professional setbacks is a powerful example of resilience in action.

- **Sheryl Sandberg:** After the sudden death of her husband, Sandberg, COO of Facebook, faced immense personal grief. Her resilience was evident as she navigated through her loss, eventually sharing her journey in her book "Option B." She emphasised the importance of building resilience by relying on support networks, practicing gratitude, and finding meaning in adversity.

Developing Emotional Strength

Emotional strength is the capacity to manage your emotions in a way that supports resilience. It involves maintaining emotional balance, being able to stay calm and composed in the face of stress and adversity, as well as being able to recover quickly from emotional setbacks.

Steps to Develop Emotional Strength:

- **Stress Management Technique:** Incorporate various stress management techniques into your routine to enhance emotional strength. Techniques such as progressive muscle relaxation, guided imagery, and deep breathing exercises can help you manage stress effectively. For example, practicing progressive muscle relaxation can help reduce physical tension and promote emotional calmness.

- **Building Emotional Endurance:** Strengthen your emotional endurance by gradually exposing yourself to challenging situations and learning to manage your responses. Gradual exposure helps you build tolerance and resilience over time. For instance, if public speaking is challenging for you, start by speaking in smaller, less intimidating settings before progressing to larger audiences.

- **Cultivating Gratitude:** Practicing gratitude can enhance emotional strength by fostering a positive mindset. Regularly acknowledging and appreciating positive aspects of your life can improve your overall outlook and emotional resilience. For example, keeping a gratitude journal where you record daily positive experiences can boost your emotional strength and resilience.

Real-Life Example:

- **Viktor Frankl:** A Holocaust survivor and psychiatrist, Frankl developed emotional strength by finding meaning in his suffering and using it to inspire others. His ability to maintain hope and resilience in the face of unimaginable adversity is a testament to the power of emotional strength.

- **Maya Angelou:** The celebrated author and poet, Maya Angelou, demonstrated immense emotional strength throughout her life, particularly in overcoming the trauma of her childhood. Her ability to channel her experiences into her writing and advocacy work exemplifies emotional resilience and strength.

Learning from Failures and Mistakes

Failure and mistakes are inevitable part of life, but how you respond to it determines your resilience. Embracing failures as learning opportunities rather than setbacks can enhance resilience and promote continuous improvement.

Strategies for Learning from Failure:

1.   Reflect on Your Experience: Take the time to reflect on your failure and identify what went wrong. What can you learn from the experience? How can you apply this knowledge to future situations? Reflection helps you gain valuable insights and prevents you from making the same mistakes again.

2.   Seek Feedback: Ask for feedback from others to gain a different perspective on your failure. Constructive feedback can help you understand where you need to improve and what you can do differently next time.

3.   Adopt a Growth Mindset: Embrace a growth mindset, which is the belief that your abilities can be developed through effort and learning. Instead of seeing failure as a dead end, view it as a steppingstone on the path to success.

4.   Move Forward: Once you've reflected on your failure and learned from it, move forward with a positive attitude. Don't dwell on the past, focus on what you can do now to improve and succeed.

Real-Life Example:

•   **J.K. Rowling:** The author of the Harry Potter series faced numerous rejections before her work was accepted by a publisher. Her ability to learn from her setbacks, persevere, and continue pursuing her passion led to her ultimate success.

11.3 Strengthening Grit

Grit is the combination of passion and perseverance that drives long-term success. Unlike talent or intelligence, grit involves sustained effort and determination over time. Strengthening grit involves cultivating passion, staying focused on long-term goals, and overcoming challenges with determination. In this section, we'll explore how to cultivate passion and perseverance, stay focused on long-term goals, and overcome challenges with determination.

How to Cultivate Passion and Perseverance

Passion and perseverance are the cornerstones of grit. Cultivating these qualities involves finding what truly excites and motivates you and maintaining commitment to your goals over the long haul.

Strategies for Cultivating Passion:

• **Pursue Meaningful Projects:** Engage in projects and activities that align with your values and long-term goals. Meaningful projects provide a sense of purpose and motivation. For example, volunteering for a cause you're passionate about can enhance your sense of purpose and commitment.

• **Connect with Like-Minded Individuals:** Surround yourself with individuals who share your interests and goals. Connecting with like-minded people can provide support, encouragement, and inspiration. For instance, joining professional associations or interest groups related to your field can help you build a network of supportive peers.

• **Set Purposeful Goals:** Establish goals that are not only achievable but also align with your passions and values. Purposeful goals provide a clear direction and motivate you to stay committed. For example, setting a goal to develop a new skill that aligns with your career aspirations can drive your perseverance and passion.

Strategies for Building Perseverance:

• **Create a Vision Statement:** Develop a personal vision statement that articulates your long-term goals and aspirations. A clear vision statement serves as a source of inspiration and motivation, helping you stay focused on your objectives. For example, a vision statement outlining your career goals and personal values can guide your decisions and actions.

• **Practice Delayed Gratification:** Cultivate the ability to delay immediate rewards for long-term benefits. Delayed gratification involves resisting short-term temptations in favour of achieving long-term goals. For instance, investing time and effort into building a career or pursuing higher education may require sacrificing immediate pleasures but can lead to greater rewards in the future.

• **Build a Support Network:** Establish a network of supportive individuals who can provide encouragement and accountability. A strong support network can help you stay motivated and persevere through challenges. For example, joining a mastermind group or finding an accountability partner can provide valuable support in achieving your goals.

Real-Life Example:

- **Malala Yousafzai:** Malala's passion for education and her perseverance in the face of extreme adversity, including being targeted by the Taliban, led her to become a global advocate for girls education. Her grit and determination exemplify the power of passion and perseverance.

- **Angela Duckworth:** As mentioned earlier, Angela Duckworth's research on grit has shown that individuals with a strong sense of passion and perseverance are more likely to achieve success. Her work emphasises the importance of staying committed to long-term goals and maintaining enthusiasm for your pursuits.

Staying Focused on Long-Term Goals

Maintaining focus on long-term goals requires discipline and persistence for achieving success. It's easy to get distracted by short-term challenges or lose motivation when progress is slow, but staying focused is key to achieving your objectives.

Strategies for Staying Focused:

- **Establish Accountability Mechanisms:** Create accountability mechanisms to track your progress and stay on course toward your goals. Accountability mechanisms can include regular check-ins with a mentor, progress reports, and goal-tracking tools. For example, using a project management app to track milestones and deadlines can help you stay organised and focused.

- **Visualise Success:** Regularly visualise achieving your long-term goals to maintain motivation and focus. Visualisation techniques involve creating mental images of your success and the steps required to achieve it. For instance, visualising the successful completion of a major project can reinforce your commitment and drive.

- **Reflect and Adjust:** Periodically reflect on your progress and adjust your strategies as needed. Regular reflection helps you stay aligned with your goals and make necessary adjustments to overcome obstacles. For example, reviewing your progress toward a career goal and adjusting your action plan based on changing circumstances can enhance your effectiveness.

Real-Life Example:

- **Oprah Winfrey:** Oprah's ability to maintain focus on her long-term goals, despite facing numerous challenges, demonstrates the importance of staying committed to one's vision. Her perseverance and focus on her career and philanthropic efforts have led to significant achievements and impact.

- **Elon Musk:** Musk's focus on long-term goals, such as colonising Mars and advancing sustainable energy, has driven his work with SpaceX and Tesla. His ability to maintain focus on his ambitious vision, despite numerous challenges, showcases the importance of staying committed to long-term goals.

- **Serena Williams:** The tennis champion Serena Williams exemplifies grit and perseverance. Her unwavering focus on her long-term goals, despite numerous setbacks and challenges, has made her one of the greatest athletes of all time.

Overcoming Challenges with Determination

Determination is the ability to persist in the face of challenges and maintain focus on your goals. Overcoming obstacles requires a combination of grit, resilience, and problem-solving skills.

Strategies for Overcoming Challenges:

- **Develop a Resilience Toolkit:** Create a toolkit of resources and strategies for managing challenges. Your resilience toolkit may include stress management techniques, coping strategies, and support resources. For example, having a list of relaxation techniques and support contacts readily available can help you navigate challenging situations more effectively.

- **Embrace Problem-Solving Mindset:** Adopt a problem-solving mindset to tackle challenges with creativity and resourcefulness. Viewing challenges as opportunities to solve problems can enhance your determination and resilience. For instance, approaching a business setback as a problem to solve rather than a failure can lead to innovative solutions and continued progress.

- **Practice Self-Compassion:** Cultivate self-compassion by treating yourself with kindness and understanding during difficult times. Self-compassion involves recognising that challenges and setbacks are part of the human experience and responding to them with empathy and support. For example, offering yourself encouragement and understanding when facing setbacks can boost your resilience and determination.

Real-Life Example:

- **Thomas Edison:** Edison's determination and persistence in the face of numerous failures and setbacks led to his ground-breaking inventions. His unwavering commitment to his goals, despite repeated failures, highlights the importance of determination in achieving success.

- **Bethany Hamilton:** After losing her arm in a shark attack, professional surfer Bethany Hamilton demonstrated incredible determination by returning to the sport she loved. Her resilience and grit have inspired many, and she continues to compete at a high level despite the challenges she faces.

Chapter 12: Improving Communication and Relationships

Communication is the cornerstone of all relationships, whether they are personal, professional, or social. Effective communication fosters understanding, trust, and connection between individuals, while poor communication can lead to misunderstandings, conflict, and the breakdown of relationships. In this chapter, we will explore the critical role communication plays in building strong relationships, the importance of active listening, and how to overcome common communication barriers. Additionally, we will delve into the development of effective communication skills, the difference between assertiveness and aggression, and strategies for navigating difficult conversations. Finally, we will discuss how to strengthen relationships by building trust, resolving conflicts, and enhancing emotional intimacy.

12.1 The Importance of Communication in Relationships

How Effective Communication Builds Strong Relationships?

Communication is the foundation upon which all relationships are built. It is the primary means through which individuals express their thoughts, feelings, and needs to one another. When communication is clear, honest, and respectful, it fosters a sense of understanding and connection between individuals. This, in turn, strengthens the bond between them and lays the groundwork for a healthy, enduring relationship.

Effective communication involves more than just speaking, it also includes listening, interpreting non-verbal cues, and being attuned to the emotions of others. When both parties in a relationship feel heard and understood, it creates a sense of mutual respect and trust. This trust is essential for building a strong relationship, as it allows individuals to feel safe in expressing their true selves without fear of judgment or rejection.

Key Aspects of Effective Communication:

1.   Clarity: Clear communication helps prevent misunderstandings. When you express your thoughts and feelings clearly, others are more likely to understand your perspective.

2.   Honesty: Being honest in your communication builds trust. When you are transparent about your thoughts and emotions, it encourages others to do the same.

3. **Empathy:** Empathetic communication involves understanding and acknowledging the feelings of others. It shows that you care about their emotional well-being and are willing to listen to their concerns.

4. **Respect:** Respectful communication involves valuing the opinions and feelings of others, even when they differ from your own. It fosters a positive and supportive environment in relationships.

Real-Life Example:

• **Michelle and Barack Obama:** The Obamas have often spoken about the importance of effective communication in their marriage. Their ability to communicate openly and honestly has been a key factor in maintaining a strong and supportive relationship, even through the challenges of public life.

The Role of Active Listening in Connection

One of the most overlooked aspects of effective communication is active listening. Many people focus so much on expressing their own thoughts that they fail to genuinely hear what others are saying. Active listening is a crucial component of effective communication. It involves fully engaging with the speaker, paying attention to their words, tone and body language, withholding judgment, and providing feedback to show understanding and empathy. It's not just about hearing the words spoken but also interpreting the underlying emotions and intent behind them.

When individuals feel heard and understood, they are more likely to open up and share their feelings, further strengthening the connection. This deep level of empathy and engagement enhances emotional intimacy and fosters an environment of trust and respect. Active listening also reduces the likelihood of misunderstandings, as it ensures that both parties are on the same page before moving forward in the conversation.

Key Techniques for Active Listening:

1.   Maintain Eye Contact: Maintaining eye contact shows that you are focused on the speaker and are fully engaged in the conversation.

2.   Nod and Use Affirmative Cues: Nodding and using phrases like "I see" or "I understand" can signal that you are following along with the conversation.

3.   Avoid Interrupting: Let the speaker finish their thoughts before responding. Interrupting can make them feel unheard and disrespected.

4.   Reflect and Clarify: Reflect back what you've heard to ensure understanding and ask questions if something is unclear.

Real-Life Example:

•   **Stephen Covey's "Seek First to Understand":** In his book "The 7 Habits of Highly Effective People," Covey emphasises the importance of active listening, suggesting that you should seek first to understand, then to be understood. This approach to communication fosters deeper connections and more meaningful relationships.

Overcoming Common Communication Barriers

While effective communication is key to building strong relationships, many communication barriers can hinder the exchange of ideas and emotions, leading to misunderstandings and conflict. These barriers can take many forms, including assumptions, emotional blocks, language differences, distractions, and lack of empathy. Overcoming these barriers requires conscious effort and self-awareness. Acknowledging and addressing these challenges is the first step toward improving communication in relationships.

Common Communication Barriers and How to Overcome Them:

1. Assumptions and Misinterpretations: Assuming you know what, the other person is thinking or feeling can lead to misunderstandings. Instead of making assumptions, ask clarifying questions to ensure you accurately understand their perspective.

2. Emotional Barriers: Strong emotions like anger, fear, or frustration can block effective communication. It's important to manage your emotions and approach conversations with a calm and open mind.

3. Language and Cultural Differences: Differences in language or cultural norms can create communication challenges. Be mindful of these differences and make an effort to understand the other person's perspective. This may involve using simple language, avoiding jargon, or being aware of cultural sensitivities.

4.   Distractions and Multitasking: Trying to communicate while distracted or multitasking can prevent you from fully engaging in the conversation. Make an effort to minimise distractions and focus on the person you are communicating with.

5.   Lack of Empathy: Failing to consider another person's perspective or emotions can cause communication breakdowns. Empathy is important for understanding and connecting with others on a deeper level.

Real-Life Example:

•   **Intercultural Communication in Business:** In global business settings, language and cultural differences can create communication barriers. Successful companies invest in cross-cultural training to help employees overcome these barriers and improve communication with colleagues and clients from diverse backgrounds.

12.2 Developing Effective Communication Skills

Verbal and Non-Verbal Communication Techniques

Effective communication is not limited to words alone, non-verbal cues such as body language, facial expressions, and tone of voice play a significant role in conveying meaning. Understanding and mastering both verbal and non-verbal communication techniques are essential for clear and impactful communication. When words and actions conflict, it can create confusion and mistrust. For example, saying "I'm fine" while crossing your arms and avoiding eye contact sends mixed signals and may lead the other person to question your true feelings.

Verbal Communication:

1.   Clarity and Precision: Use clear and precise language to convey your message. Avoid ambiguity and be specific about your needs, thoughts, and feelings.

2.   Tone of Voice: Your tone of voice can significantly impact how your message is received. A calm and friendly tone fosters positive interactions, while a harsh or sarcastic tone can lead to misunderstandings and conflict.

3.   Pacing and Pausing: The speed at which you speak can affect the listener's ability to understand your message. Speaking too quickly may overwhelm the listener, while pausing at appropriate moments can emphasise key points and allow the listener to absorb the information.

Non-Verbal Communication:

1.   Body Language: Your posture, gestures, and facial expressions can communicate your emotions and intentions. Open and relaxed body language conveys approachability and confidence, while crossed arms or avoiding eye contact may signal defensiveness or discomfort.

2.   Facial Expressions: Your facial expressions can reveal your true feelings, even when your words do not. Smiling, for example, can convey friendliness and warmth, while frowning may indicate disapproval or frustration.

3.   Eye Contact: Maintaining eye contact shows that you are engaged and attentive. It also helps build trust and rapport with the person you are communicating with.

Real-Life Example:

•   **Politicians and Public Speaking:** Politicians often use both verbal and non-verbal communication techniques to connect with their audience. For example, during speeches, they may use gestures to emphasise points, maintain eye contact to engage with the audience, and modulate their tone to convey passion or concern.

Assertiveness vs. Aggression

Assertiveness is a communication style that allows individuals to express their thoughts, needs, feelings and opinions in a direct, honest, respectful, and confident manner. It is often confused with aggression, but the two are vastly different. While aggression involves dominating or controlling others through forceful behaviour, assertiveness strikes a balance between passivity and aggression.

Being assertive means standing up for yourself without disregarding or harming others. It involves expressing your views clearly and respectfully, while also being open to hearing and understanding the other person's perspective. Assertive communication strengthens relationships because it fosters mutual respect and prevents resentment from building up. On the other hand, aggression involves expressing yourself in a way that violates the rights of others, often through hostility or intimidation.

Key Differences Between Assertiveness and Aggression:

1.   **Respect for Others:** Assertive communication respects both your own rights and the rights of others. Aggressive communication, however, prioritises your needs at the expense of others.

2.   **Tone and Delivery:** Assertive communication is calm, clear, and confident, while aggressive communication is often loud, confrontational, and disrespectful.

3. **Outcome:** Assertive communication tends to lead to positive outcomes, such as mutual understanding and problem-solving. Aggressive communication, on the other hand, often leads to conflict and damaged relationships.

Strategies for Being More Assertive:

1. **Use "I" Statements:** Frame your thoughts and feelings in terms of "I" statements, such as "I feel" or "I need," rather than blaming others. For example, say "I feel frustrated when my ideas are ignored" instead of "You never listen to me."

2. **Be Direct and Honest:** Clearly state your needs and expectations without beating around the bush. Avoid passive-aggressive behaviour or hinting at what you want.

3. **Practice Saying No:** Assertiveness involves setting boundaries and saying no when necessary. Practice declining requests that do not align with your priorities or values.

Real-Life Example:

• **Workplace Communication:** In the workplace, being assertive can help you advocate for yourself, whether it's asking for a raise, setting boundaries with colleagues, or expressing concerns. Assertive communication fosters respect and collaboration, while aggressive communication can create tension and conflict.

Navigating Difficult Conversations

Difficult conversations are an inevitable part of any relationship, but they don't have to be destructive. Whether it's addressing a conflict, delivering bad news, discussing sensitive topics, or providing constructive feedback, approaching these tough conversations with empathy and clarity can prevent misunderstandings and strengthen your relationships.

Strategies for Navigating Difficult Conversations:

1.   **Prepare Ahead of Time:** Before initiating a difficult conversation, take the time to gather your thoughts and goals. What do you hope to achieve from the conversation? Being clear about your intentions can help guide the discussion in a productive direction.

2.   **Stay Calm and Composed:** Emotional intensity can derail difficult conversations. If emotions can run high during difficult conversations, it's important to stay calm and composed. Take deep breaths, and if you feel yourself becoming emotional, pause and collect your thoughts before continuing.

3.   **Acknowledge the Other Person's Perspective:** During the conversation, make an effort to listen actively to the other person's perspective. Demonstrating that you understand the other person's feelings and concerns helps build trust and can defuse tension. Avoid interrupting or becoming defensive and acknowledge their feelings and concerns. Even if you don't agree, validating their perspective shows respect.

4.   Focus on Solutions: Rather than dwelling on the problem, focus on finding a solution that works for both parties. Approach the conversation with a collaborative mindset and be open to compromise.

Real-Life Example:

•   **Mediation in Conflict Resolution:** In legal or workplace disputes, mediators often facilitate difficult conversations between conflicting parties. Their goal is to guide the conversation in a way that allows both sides to be heard and to find a mutually acceptable resolution.

12.3 Strengthening Relationships

Building Trust and Mutual Respect

Trust is the cornerstone of any healthy relationship, and it's built through consistent, open, and honest communication. Trust doesn't happen overnight; it is earned through repeated actions that demonstrate reliability, empathy, and integrity. Once trust is established, it creates a safe space for individuals to be vulnerable, express their true feelings, and rely on one another.

Mutual respect, on the other hand, involves recognising and appreciating the worth and dignity of the other person. In relationships, respect means valuing each other's opinions, emotions, and boundaries, even when there are disagreements. Trust and respect go hand in hand, and both are essential for long-lasting, meaningful relationships.

Strategies for Building Trust:

1. **Be Reliable:** Consistency is key to building trust. Follow through on your promises, be dependable, and show that you can be counted on in both good times and bad.

2. **Communicate Openly:** Open and honest communication is key to building trust. Be transparent about your thoughts, feelings, and intentions, and encourage the other person to do the same. Avoiding dishonesty or withholding information strengthens the bond of trust between individuals.

3. **Show Empathy:** Demonstrating empathy shows that you genuinely care about the other person's feelings and well-being. This helps build a strong emotional connection, respect, and deepens trust.

4. **Respect Boundaries:** Respecting the other person's boundaries and privacy is crucial for building mutual respect. Avoid overstepping boundaries or pressuring them into situations that make them uncomfortable.

Real-Life Example:

• **Trust in Marriage:** In a marriage, trust is essential for maintaining a strong partnership. Couples who communicate openly, support each other, and respect each other's boundaries are more likely to build a lasting and fulfilling relationship.

Conflict Resolution and Compromise

Conflict is a natural part of any relationship, but how conflicts are handled can determine the health and longevity of the relationship. Effective conflict resolution involves addressing disagreements in a constructive manner and finding compromises that satisfy both parties.

Strategies for Conflict Resolution:

1.   Address the Issue Early: Don't let conflicts fester. Address issues as soon as they arise to prevent them from escalating into larger problems.

2.   Stay Focused on the Issue: When resolving conflicts, it is important to stay focused on the issue at hand and avoid bringing up past grievances or making personal attacks. This keeps the conversation productive and avoid escalating the conflict.

3.   Seek to Understand: Before defending your position, take the time to understand the other person's perspective. This can help de-escalate the situation and pave the way for a more productive conversation.

4.   Use "I" Statements: Expressing your feelings using "I" statements (e.g., "I feel hurt when...") prevents the other person from feeling attacked and makes it easier to resolve the issue without defensiveness.

5.   Be Willing to Compromise: Healthy relationships require compromise. Rather than trying to "win" the argument, both parties should seek a resolution that meets both of their needs. Compromise doesn't mean one person gives in entirely; rather, it involves finding a middle ground that works for both parties.

Real-Life Example:

•   **Mediation in Relationships:** In some cases, couples or colleagues may seek the help of a mediator to resolve conflicts. Mediators facilitate discussions and help both parties find common ground, leading to a resolution that is acceptable to all involved.

Enhancing Emotional Intimacy

Emotional intimacy is the deep connection that allows individuals to share their innermost thoughts and feelings with each other. It is the foundation of closeness that goes beyond physical proximity and is marked by trust, vulnerability, and shared experiences. Enhancing emotional intimacy requires regular and meaningful communication, as well as a willingness to be vulnerable with each other.

Strategies for Enhancing Emotional Intimacy:

1.   Be Vulnerable: Emotional intimacy requires vulnerability. Being open and honest about your feelings, fears, and desires creates a space for deeper connection. When individuals feel safe expressing their true selves, it fosters emotional closeness.

2. **Spend Quality Time Together:** Emotional intimacy is built through shared experiences and meaningful interactions. Making time to connect on a deeper level, without destructions, strengthens the bond. This can involve engaging in activities together, having meaningful conversations, or simply being present with one another.

3. **Express Appreciation:** Regularly express appreciation and gratitude for the other person. Acknowledging their contributions and showing that you value them strengthens your emotional connection.

4. **Practice Active Listening:** Active listening fosters emotional intimacy by showing that you are fully engaged and supportive of the other person's feelings and experiences.

Real-Life Example:

• **Close Friendships:** In close friendships, emotional intimacy is often what sets the relationship apart from more casual acquaintances. Friends who share their innermost thoughts and feelings, support each other through challenges, and spend quality time together tend to have stronger, more fulfilling relationships.

Chapter 13: Forgiveness and Letting Go of Grudges

Forgiveness is a profound and transformative act, an essential step toward healing, and a powerful release from the burdens that hold us back. It goes beyond simply saying the words "I forgive you". It is a choice to free ourselves from the weight of resentment and anger, to find inner peace, and to move forward without the chains of past hurts. In this chapter, we will explore what forgiveness truly means, the process of forgiving others and ourselves, and the freedom that comes with letting go of grudges.

13.1 Understanding Forgiveness

What Forgiveness Is and Isn't

Forgiveness is often misunderstood, so it's essential to clarify what forgiveness truly entails. Forgiveness is a conscious, deliberate decision to release feelings of resentment or vengeance toward someone who has harmed you, regardless of whether they deserve your forgiveness. This definition emphasises that forgiveness is an internal process that does not necessarily require reconciliation with the person who wronged you. It is about freeing yourself from the emotional burden that comes with holding onto grudges.

It is crucial to recognise that forgiveness does not mean condoning or excusing harmful behaviour. It doesn't mean forgetting what happened or denying the hurt that you experienced. Instead, forgiveness is about acknowledging the pain, accepting that it occurred, and choosing to let go of the negative emotions associated with it. By doing so, you allow yourself to heal and move forward without being tethered to the past.

Forgiveness also does not require an apology from the person who wronged you. While an apology may facilitate the forgiveness process, it is not a prerequisite. Forgiveness is a personal journey that you undertake for your own well-being, regardless of the actions or inactions of others.

The Emotional and Psychological Benefits of Forgiveness

The emotional and psychological benefits of forgiveness are profound. Holding onto grudges and resentment can lead to chronic stress, anxiety, and even depression. These negative emotions can permeate every aspect of your life, affecting your relationships, work, and overall sense of well-being. By forgiving, you release these toxic emotions and create space for healing and growth.

Forgiveness can also lead to improved mental clarity. When you are consumed by anger and resentment, it can be challenging to think clearly and make rational decisions. Forgiveness allows you to regain control over your thoughts and emotions, leading to better decision-making and problem-solving abilities.

Moreover, forgiveness can enhance your self-esteem and sense of self-worth. When you forgive, you affirm that you are worthy of peace and happiness. You acknowledge that your well-being is more important than holding onto past grievances. This shift in perspective can lead to greater self-acceptance and confidence.

Myths About Forgiveness

There are several common myths about forgiveness that can create barriers to the forgiveness process. Understanding these myths is essential to developing a healthier approach to forgiveness. Some of the most common myths include:

- **Forgiveness means forgetting.** Forgiveness does not require you to forget what happened. In fact, it's essential to acknowledge and process the hurt in order to truly forgive. The goal is not to erase the memory but to remove the emotional charge associated with it.

- **Forgiveness is a sign of weakness.** Forgiving someone doesn't make you weak; In reality, forgiveness requires immense strength and courage. It takes resilience to face your pain, let go of anger, and choose compassion instead. Forgiveness is not about giving in or being passive, it is an active and empowering choice to prioritise your well-being.

- **Forgiveness happens all at once.** Forgiveness is often a gradual process. It may take time to fully release the negative emotions tied to a specific event or person. It's important to be patient with yourself as you work through the stages of forgiveness.

- **Forgiveness means excusing the behaviour.** Forgiving someone doesn't mean you condone their actions or absolve them of responsibility. It's about freeing yourself from the emotional burden, not excusing the behaviour.

- **You have to forgive in order to heal.** While forgiveness can be a powerful tool for healing, it's not always necessary for everyone. Healing can take many forms, and forgiveness is just one path. If you're not ready to forgive, it's okay to focus on other aspects of your healing journey.

•   **Forgiveness must be immediate.** In truth, forgiveness is often a gradual process that takes time. It is okay to take the time you need to process your emotions and arrive at a place of forgiveness. Forcing yourself to forgive prematurely can be counterproductive and may lead to unresolved feelings resurfacing later on.

•   **Forgiving others means they must reconcile with them.** While reconciliation can be a positive outcome of forgiveness, it is not always necessary or advisable. You can forgive someone without re-establishing a relationship with them, especially if the relationship was harmful or toxic.

13.2 The Process of Forgiveness

Steps to Forgiving Others

Forgiving someone who has wronged you can be a challenging process, but it is ultimately a path to inner peace. The following steps can help guide you through the process of forgiveness:

1.   **Acknowledge the Hurt:** The first step in forgiveness is acknowledging the hurt and allowing yourself to feel the emotions associated with it. Denying or suppressing your emotions or feelings can hinder the forgiveness process and prevent healing. It's essential to give yourself permission to grieve, feel anger, or experience whatever emotions arise.

2.   Understand the Impact: Reflect on how holding onto the hurt and anger is impacting your life. Is it preventing you from moving forward? Is it affecting your relationships or your mental and emotional well-being? Understanding the consequences of holding onto grudges can motivate you to let go.

3.   Empathise with the Offender: This step can be difficult, but it's crucial for forgiveness. Try to see the situation from the other person's perspective. What were their motivations? Were they acting out of their own pain, insecurities, or limitation? Empathy doesn't mean excusing their behaviour, but it can help you understand why they acted the way they did, and it can also help you move toward forgiveness.

4.   Decide to Forgive: Forgiveness is a conscious choice. Once you've acknowledged the hurt and empathised with the offender, decide whether you're ready to forgive. This decision is for your own peace of mind, not for the benefit of the other person.

5.   Release the Grudge: Letting go of the grudge involves releasing the negative emotions tied to the event. This can be done through various methods, such as journaling, meditation, or talking to a trusted friend or therapist. The goal is to process your emotions in a healthy way and gradually let go of the anger, resentment, and desire for revenge.

6.   Focus on the Present: Once you've let go of the grudge, it's important to focus on the present. Don't dwell on the past or the hurt. Instead, channel your energy into positive experiences and relationships.

Forgiving Yourself for Past Mistakes

Self-forgiveness is just as important as forgiving others, yet it is often more challenging. Many people hold themselves to impossibly high standards and struggle to let go of guilt and shame over past mistakes. However, self-forgiveness is essential for personal growth and emotional well-being.

1.   **Acknowledge Your Mistakes:** Just as with forgiving others, the first step in self-forgiveness is acknowledging your mistakes. It's important to accept responsibility for your actions without minimising or rationalising them. This does not mean dwelling on the mistake or engaging in self-punishment, but rather accepting that you are human and capable of error.

2.   **Recognise Your Humanity:** Understand that everyone makes mistakes. You are not alone in your shortcomings. Recognising your humanity and the inevitability of making mistakes can help you approach yourself with compassion.

3.   **Identify the Lesson:** Mistakes offer valuable lessons. Reflect on what you've learned from the experience and how it has helped you grow as a person. By focusing on the lessons, you can transform your mistakes into opportunities for growth.

4.   **Practice Self-Compassion:** Treat yourself with the same kindness and understanding that you would offer a friend who made a mistake. Self-compassion involves recognising your pain, offering yourself comfort, and encouraging yourself to move forward.

5. **Let Go of Guilt:** Guilt can be a heavy burden to carry, and it often serves no constructive purpose. Once you've acknowledged your mistakes and learned from them, it's time to let go of the guilt. Holding onto guilt only keeps you stuck in the past.

6. **Make Amends:** If your actions have hurt others, making amends can be an important part of self-forgiveness. Apologise sincerely, and if possible, take steps to right the wrong. This can help you release any lingering guilt and move forward with a clear conscience.

Letting Go of Resentment and Anger

Resentment and anger are powerful emotions that can consume your thoughts and negatively impact your life. These emotions can be deeply ingrained and difficult to release, but holding onto them only prolongs your suffering. Letting go of these emotions is essential for your well-being and personal growth.

1. **Acknowledge Your Resentment:** Start by acknowledging your resentment and anger. Identify the source of these emotions and how they are affecting your life. This awareness is the first step toward letting go.

2. **Challenge Your Thoughts:** Resentment often stems from thoughts that reinforce your anger, such as replaying the hurtful event in your mind or believing that the other person "deserves" your anger. Challenge these thoughts by asking yourself whether they are helping you or holding you back.

3.   Shift Your Focus: Instead of focusing on the person or event that caused your resentment, shift your focus to the positive aspects of your life. Gratitude practices can be particularly helpful in redirecting your attention away from negative emotions.

4.   Engaged in Activities: It can be helpful to engage in activities that promote emotional release, such as physical exercise, creative expression, or spending time in nature. These activities can help you process and release pent-up emotions in a healthy way.

5.   Reframe your Perspective: Instead of focusing on the injustice of what happened, try to see the situation as an opportunity for growth and learning. This shift in mindset can help you move from place of victimhood to empowerment.

6.   Practice Mindfulness: Mindfulness can help you stay present and preventing yourself from getting caught up in negative thoughts and reduce the intensity of your anger. Mindfulness allows you to observe your feelings without judgement and gradually release them.

7.   Release the Need for Justice: Resentment often stems from a desire for justice or retribution. Letting go of this need can be liberating. Accept that you may never get the resolution or apology you desire, and that's okay. Your peace of mind is more important.

8.   Forgive, Even If It's Hard: Letting go of resentment requires forgiveness, even if it's difficult. Remember that forgiveness is for your benefit, not the other person's. It's about freeing yourself from the emotional burden of holding onto anger.

9.   **Seek Support:** Consider seeking support from a therapist or counsellor. Sometimes, professional guidance is necessary to work through deep-seated anger and resentment. A therapist can provide tools and strategies to help you let go of these emotions and move toward forgiveness.

13.3 The Freedom of Letting Go

How Letting Go of Grudges Leads to Healing

Letting go of grudges is a liberating experience that can lead to profound healing. When you hold onto a grudge, you keep yourself trapped in a cycle of negativity. This emotional baggage can weigh you down and prevent you from fully enjoying life. By letting go, you free yourself from the past and create space for new, positive experiences.

Healing begins when you release the need for revenge or retribution. Holding onto a grudge often involves a desire to see the other person suffer in the same way you did. However, this mindset only perpetuates your own suffering. Letting go allows you to break free from this cycle and focus on your own well-being.

Letting go of grudges also promotes physical healing. Research has shown that chronic anger and resentment can contribute to various health issues, including high blood pressure, heart disease, and a weakened immune system. By releasing these negative emotions, you can improve your physical health and overall quality of life.

Additionally, letting go of grudges can lead to improved relationships. When you are no longer consumed by past hurts, you can approach your interactions with others with greater openness and compassion. This can strengthen your connections and create more harmonious relationships.

The Role of Compassion in Forgiveness

Compassion is a powerful tool in the forgiveness process. It involves extending understanding and kindness toward both yourself and others. When you approach forgiveness with compassion, you are more likely to release the anger and resentment that keep you stuck in the past. Compassion allows you to see beyond the hurt and recognise the humanity in others. It helps you understand that people make mistakes, often due to their own pain, insecurities, or limited understanding, which can help you move toward forgiveness.

Practicing self-compassion is equally important. When you forgive yourself, you acknowledge that you are worthy of peace and happiness. Self-compassion helps you let go of guilt and shame and allows you to focus on personal growth and healing.

Compassion also plays a crucial role in letting go of grudges. When you approach others with compassion, you are more likely to release the need for revenge or retribution. Instead, you can focus on healing and moving forward.

Finally, compassion can help you maintain forgiveness over time. Forgiveness is not always a one-time event, it is often an ongoing process. By continually practicing compassion, you can reinforce your commitment to forgiveness and prevent old hurts from resurfacing.

Moving Forward with Peace and Clarity

Moving forward with peace and clarity is the ultimate goal of forgiveness. Once you have forgiven and let go of grudges, you can begin to move forward with a sense of peace and clarity. This new perspective allows you to approach life with a lighter heart and a more open mind. You are no longer burdened by the weight of past hurts, and you can focus on creating positive experiences in the present.

Moving forward with peace and clarity also come from accepting the past and embracing the lessons you've learned through the process of forgiveness. Every experience, no matter how painful, offers opportunity for growth and self-improvement. These lessons can help you navigate future challenges with greater resilience and wisdom. You may find that you are more compassionate, understanding, and patient with both yourself and others.

Living with peace and clarity also means letting go of the need to control or change others. You cannot control what others do, but you can control how you respond. By focusing on your own well-being and letting go of the need for external validation or retribution, you can find true inner peace.

As you move forward with peace and clarity, it's important to remember that forgiveness is an ongoing process that requires practice and dedication. There may be moments when old hurts resurface, and that's okay. The key is to continue practicing forgiveness and letting go, trusting that each step brings you closer to a more peaceful and fulfilling life.

Chapter 14: Navigating Life Transitions

Life is filled with inevitable changes, from predictable milestones to unforeseen challenges. These transitions, while sometimes daunting, shape the journey of life. They provide opportunities for personal growth, renewal, and transformation. Navigating these changes with resilience and a positive mindset allows us to better cope with uncertainty and embrace new beginnings.

In this chapter, we will delve into the nature of life transitions, how to cope with them effectively, and how to thrive through change. By understanding the emotional and psychological aspects of transitions and implementing strategies for resilience and growth, individuals can navigate life's changes with more confidence and purpose.

14.1 The Nature of Life Transitions

Understanding Major Life Transitions

Life transitions are periods of significant change, whether expected or unexpected, that require an individual to adjust to new circumstances. These transitions encompass a broad range of experiences, from personal milestones like getting married, having children, or retiring, to more difficult changes such as losing a job, moving to a new city, or the passing of a loved one.

Transitions can be classified into two categories: planned transitions and unplanned transitions.

- **Planned transitions** include events such as graduating from school, moving into a new home, or advancing in your career. These changes are often anticipated, and while they may still cause stress or uncertainty, they typically come with an element of preparation.

- **Unplanned transitions**, on the other hand, include events like an unexpected job loss, a breakup, or a sudden illness. These types of transitions often leave individuals feeling unprepared, creating additional emotional challenges.

What makes transitions particularly impactful is the disruption they cause to our routines, relationships, and identity. Even positive changes, like starting a new job or entering into a committed relationship, can evoke feelings of anxiety as they push us out of our comfort zones and into unfamiliar territory. The process of navigating through these changes requires us to adjust our mindset, routines, and expectations to align with the new realities we face.

Transitions also challenge our sense of control over life's circumstances. During times of change, it's common to feel like you've lost control over certain aspects of your life, which can increase feelings of vulnerability and stress. However, recognising that life is filled with change both good and bad can help individuals mentally prepare for and accept transitions when they occur.

The Emotional Impact of Change

The emotional impact of life transitions varies depending on the nature and magnitude of the change. Regardless of whether a transition is perceived as positive or negative, it can lead to a complex array of emotions. These emotions may include excitement, anxiety, fear, sadness, hope, and even relief.

One of the most significant emotions experienced during a life transition is uncertainty. When transitioning to a new phase of life, the future can feel unclear, and the unknown can be unsettling. This uncertainty often leads to feelings of anxiety as individuals grapple with the question, "What happens next?" Even in cases where the outcome of a transition is positive, such as a promotion or marriage, the unpredictability of new circumstances can evoke stress.

Life transitions may also trigger grief and a sense of loss. While grief is often associated with the loss of a loved one, it can also arise during other transitions, such as retiring from a fulfilling career, selling a home where many memories were made, or ending a long-term relationship. Grief in these situations stems from the sense of loss of the past or the familiar. These feelings of loss can make transitions more challenging to navigate emotionally.

Another emotional aspect of life transitions is identity reconstruction. Many significant life changes challenge our self-concept and how we see ourselves in the world. For example, when someone retires after many years of working, they may struggle to redefine themselves outside of their professional role. Similarly, becoming a parent or entering a new relationship can challenge an individual's sense of independence. During these transitions, it's common to question, "Who am I now?" Rebuilding a sense of identity in the context of a new reality can be a daunting but essential aspect of adapting to change.

The Growth Opportunities in Transitions

While transitions can be emotionally challenging, they also provide opportunities for personal growth, self-discovery, and transformation. Change, though uncomfortable, is often the catalyst for development. By stepping outside of our comfort zones, we are encouraged to explore new perspectives, develop new skills, and gain a deeper understanding of ourselves.

Life transitions often serve as a time of reflection and reassessment. When faced with change, we are forced to pause and evaluate our current circumstances, relationships, goals, and values. This process can lead to a deeper sense of self-awareness and provide clarity about what we truly want in life. For example, during a career change, you might reflect on what brings you joy and fulfillment in your work, leading to a more aligned and purposeful career path.

Furthermore, transitions challenge us to build resilience. Resilience is the ability to adapt and recover from adversity, and it is often strengthened through the process of navigating life's ups and downs. Each time we successfully navigate a difficult transition, we become better equipped to handle future challenges. This capacity for resilience empowers us to face uncertainty with confidence and to see change as an opportunity for growth rather than a threat.

14.2 Coping with Change

Techniques for Managing Uncertainty

Uncertainty is an inherent aspect of any life transition, and learning to manage it effectively is essential for maintaining emotional well-being during times of change. While uncertainty can trigger fear and anxiety, there are several strategies you can employ to cope with the unknown.

One of the most effective techniques for managing uncertainty is to focus on what you can control. While many aspects of a transition may be beyond your influence, there are always elements within your control. By identifying and focusing on these areas, you can regain a sense of agency and reduce feelings of helplessness. For example, if you are transitioning to a new job, you may not be able to control how quickly you adapt to the role, but you can control how prepared you are by researching the company, improving your skills, and maintaining a positive attitude.

Another key strategy is to practice mindfulness and staying present in the moment. Anxiety often stems from worrying about future outcomes, and mindfulness can help you redirect your attention to the present, reducing the impact of uncertainty on your mental state. Simple mindfulness practices, such as deep breathing exercises, meditation, or focusing on the sensations in your body, can help ground you and alleviate feelings of overwhelm.

Additionally, maintaining a flexible mindset can help you navigate the unpredictability of life transitions. Rather than clinging to rigid expectations about how things should unfold, try to remain open to different outcomes and possibilities. Life rarely goes exactly as planned, and the ability to adapt and adjust your expectations is crucial for managing transitions effectively.

Building Resilience During Transitions

Resilience is the ability to bounce back from challenges, and it is an essential trait for navigating life transitions successfully. Building resilience during transitions requires cultivating mental and emotional strength, as well as developing strategies for managing stress and adversity.

One way to build resilience is to reframe the way you view challenges. Rather than seeing a transition as a setback or obstacle, try to view it as an opportunity for growth and self-improvement. This shift in perspective can help reduce feelings of defeat or frustration and motivate you to take proactive steps toward overcoming the challenges associated with the transition.

Another key to building resilience is practicing self-care. Transitions can be emotionally and physically draining, so it's important to prioritise activities that nourish your body and mind. Exercise, healthy eating, sufficient sleep, and relaxation techniques all contribute to a sense of well-being and help build the physical and emotional stamina needed to navigate change.

Seeking support from others is also a critical component of building resilience. Whether it's talking to a trusted friend, family member, or professional therapist, sharing your feelings and experiences with others can provide valuable perspective and emotional relief. It's important to remember that you don't have to navigate life transitions alone, and reaching out for support can help you build the resilience needed to cope with change.

Seeking Support and Guidance

Navigating a life transition can feel overwhelming, and seeking support from others is essential for emotional and mental well-being. Having a strong support system can provide you with encouragement, advice, and a sense of belonging during times of uncertainty.

Emotional support from friends and family can help you process the complex feelings that arise during transitions. Simply talking about your experiences and emotions can provide relief and help you gain clarity about your situation. Loved ones can offer comfort, perspective, and reassurance that you are not alone in your journey.

In some cases, professional guidance may be necessary to navigate particularly difficult transitions. A therapist or counsellor can provide you with the tools and strategies to cope with the emotional challenges of change. They can help you explore your feelings, identify underlying patterns, and develop a plan for moving forward.

Support groups, whether in-person or online, can also be valuable resources during life transitions. These groups provide a space to connect with others who are going through similar experiences, offering empathy, and understanding. Sharing your journey with others who can relate to your struggles can provide a sense of camaraderie and hope.

14.3 Embracing New Beginnings

Finding Opportunity in Change

Change, while difficult, often brings new opportunities for growth and fulfillment. Embracing new beginnings requires a shift in perspective, moving from fear and resistance to curiosity and openness. By seeing change as a chance to explore new possibilities, you can approach transitions with a sense of optimism and excitement.

One of the most effective ways to find opportunity in change is to set new goals and intentions. Transitions provide a natural opportunity to reassess your priorities and create a vision for your future. For example, if you are transitioning into a new career, take the time to reflect on what truly brings you joy and fulfillment in your work. Use this reflection to set goals that align with your values and aspirations.

Staying curious and open to new experiences is another way to embrace new beginnings. Life transitions often require stepping out of your comfort zone and trying new things. Whether it's learning a new skill, meeting new people, or exploring new interests, approaching these experiences with curiosity can help you find joy and meaning in the midst of change.

Rebuilding After Loss or Transition

Loss is an inevitable part of life, and transitions often involve some form of loss whether it's the loss of a loved one, a job, or a way of life. Rebuilding after loss requires time, patience, and self-compassion. It's important to acknowledge and process the grief that comes with loss before you can begin to rebuild.

Rebuilding after loss involves creating a new sense of identity and purpose. This may involve letting go of old expectations or roles and embracing a new chapter of life. While the process of rebuilding can be painful, it also provides an opportunity for personal growth and renewal.

One key to rebuilding after loss is to focus on what remains rather than what has been lost. While transitions often involve letting go of something, they also provide new opportunities for growth and fulfillment. By focusing on the positive aspects of your new circumstances, you can begin to rebuild a life that is meaningful and fulfilling.

Thriving in Your Next Chapter

Thriving through transitions means more than just surviving, it's about embracing the changes and using them as a catalyst for personal growth and fulfillment. To thrive in your next chapter, it's important to cultivate a mindset of resilience, optimism, and self-compassion.

One key to thriving is to stay open to new experiences and opportunities. Life transitions often involve stepping into the unknown, and it's important to approach this next phase with a sense of curiosity and adventure. Whether it's trying new activities, meeting new people, or exploring new interests, staying open to new possibilities can help you find joy and fulfillment in this next chapter.

Another important aspect of thriving is to stay connected to your values and sense of purpose. Life transitions can sometimes leave us feeling unmoored or uncertain about our direction, but staying grounded in your values can provide you with a sense of stability and meaning. Reflect on what matters most to you and use your values as a guide as you move forward into this new phase of life.

Finally, thriving in your next chapter requires self-compassion and patience. Transitions take time, and it's important to give yourself grace as you adjust to the changes. Celebrate your progress, no matter how small, and remember that thriving is not about perfection it's about embracing the journey and growing through the process.

Chapter 15: Overcoming Procrastination and Perfectionism

Procrastination and perfectionism are two challenges that, when left unchecked, can hinder personal growth, productivity, and success. Procrastination, the act of delaying tasks or decisions, and perfectionism, the relentless pursuit of flawlessness, are deeply intertwined. Many individuals find themselves trapped in a cycle of putting off tasks out of fear that the results won't be perfect, leading to both stress and stagnation.

In this chapter, we will delve into the reasons behind procrastination and perfectionism and explore practical techniques to break free from these patterns. By understanding the emotional and psychological roots of these behaviours and applying actionable strategies, individuals can cultivate a healthier mindset and achieve their goals without unnecessary stress.

15.1 Understanding Procrastination

Why We Procrastinate

Procrastination is not simply about being lazy or avoiding responsibility. Instead, it often reflects deeper emotional and psychological patterns. Understanding why we procrastinate is the first step toward overcoming it.

Reasons Why People Procrastinate

• **Fear of failure:** One of the most common reasons for procrastination is the fear of failing. Fear can manifest in various forms: fear of failure, fear of judgment, or even fear of success. When we fear that our efforts won't meet expectations, we may avoid starting tasks altogether. This avoidance provides temporary relief from anxiety but often leads to greater stress as deadlines loom closer.

• **Feeling overwhelmed:** When a task feels too large or complex, it can be difficult to know where to start. This paralysis leads to postponing the task, which only makes it seem more daunting over time. The larger the task appears, the more overwhelming it becomes, and this cycle continues until external pressure, like a looming deadline, forces action.

• **Lack of motivation:** Another major contributor to procrastination. When a task doesn't align with our values or interests, or when the immediate reward for completing it is unclear, it becomes easy to put it off. Without a clear sense of purpose or intrinsic motivation, we might struggle to muster the energy or enthusiasm to begin.

- **Perfectionism:** Plays a significant role in procrastination. Perfectionists often delay starting tasks because they fear they won't be able to execute them perfectly. This creates a self-perpetuating loop. The longer the task is delayed, the less time there is to complete it to perfection, which increases anxiety and leads to further procrastination.

The Emotional and Psychological Roots of Procrastination

Procrastination can often be traced back to emotional responses and psychological mechanisms. It is a behaviour that provides short-term relief from uncomfortable feelings but creates long-term stress and dissatisfaction. Here are some of the emotional roots of procrastination:

- **Fear of failure:** Procrastination is a defence mechanism against the fear of failing. The thought of failing or not meeting expectations can be so paralysing that people choose to delay action, as this allows them to avoid confronting the possibility of falling short of their own or other's expectations.

- **Low self-esteem:** This can also contribute to procrastination. When individuals who doubt their abilities or believe they are not capable of success, they may put off tasks as a way of avoiding confirmation of these negative beliefs. This leads to a self-reinforcing cycle of delay and avoidance, further damaging self-esteem.

• **Stress and anxiety:** People may procrastinate because they are already feeling overwhelmed or anxious, and avoiding the task provides temporary relief from these emotions. Unfortunately, the longer the task is postponed, the more anxiety and stress build, creating a vicious cycle.

• **Decision paralysis:** Some people struggle with making decisions, especially when faced with multiple choices or uncertain outcomes. The fear of making the wrong choice can result in indecision, causing them to put off the task entirely.

The Consequences of Procrastination

While procrastination might provide short-term relief from stress or anxiety, it often leads to negative consequences in the long run:

• **Increased stress.** As deadlines approach, the pressure to complete the task intensifies, often resulting in panic, rushed work, and subpar results. The stress of procrastination not only affects productivity but also negatively impacts mental health, leading to feelings of guilt, shame, and frustration.

• **Erosion of Self-confidence.** Each time an individual procrastinates and fails to meet deadlines or achieve goals, they reinforce a negative self-image. This perpetuates a cycle where low self-esteem leads to procrastination, and procrastination, in turn, diminishes confidence even further.

- **Negative impact on success.** Missed deadlines, lost promotions, incomplete projects, and an inability to follow through on commitments can lead to lost opportunities, damaged reputations, and strained relationships. Over time, chronic procrastination can prevent individuals from reaching their full potential, both personally and professionally.

- **Loss of peace of mind.** The constant pressure of unfinished tasks hanging over one's head creates mental clutter, making it difficult to focus on the present moment or enjoy leisure time. The inability to relax, coupled with the growing to-do list, contributes to a sense of never-ending anxiety.

15.2 Techniques to Overcome Procrastination

Now that we understand the roots and consequences of procrastination, let's explore techniques to overcome it and build productive habits.

Breaking Tasks into Smaller Steps

One of the most effective techniques for overcoming procrastination is to break large tasks down into smaller, manageable steps. When a task seems overwhelming, it's easy to avoid it altogether. By breaking the task into smaller components, each step reduces the feeling of overwhelm and makes it more achievable and less intimidating. Here's how to do it:

- **Create a clear action plan:** Start by creating an outline. Once the outline is complete, focus on writing the introduction. Break down the task into bite-sized pieces makes it easier to start, and once you've completed one small step, it builds momentum to continue. For instance, instead of focusing on writing an entire report, start by outlining the key points.

- **Set micro-goals:** These are small, easily achievable goals that can be accomplished in a short period. By focusing on these micro-goals, you can trick your brain into thinking the task isn't as big as it seems. Completing each micro-goal provides a sense of accomplishment, which boosts motivation to keep going.

- **Celebrate small wins:** Acknowledge and celebrate the completion of each step. This boosts motivation and encourages further progress.
For example, if you're procrastinating on cleaning your house, instead of cleaning the whole house at once, start by organising just one room or one part of a room. Breaking down the task reduces the sense of overwhelm.

Using Deadlines and Accountability

Deadlines and accountability systems are powerful tools for overcoming procrastination:

- **Set self-imposed deadlines:** Creating self-imposed deadlines can be a powerful motivator to overcome procrastination. Deadlines create a sense of urgency and provide structure to your time. To make these deadlines effective, it is important to treat them as seriously as external deadlines. Adding specific time and dates for completion makes them more tangible and harder to ignore. For example, "I'll finish writing the introduction by noon."

- **Share your goals:** Accountability can play a crucial role in combating procrastination. When you know someone else is counting on you or aware of your progress, you're more likely to stay committed. This is where accountability partners come in whether it's a friend, colleague, coach or family member, sharing your goals and check-ins regularly can provide motivation and encouragement.

- **Join an accountability group:** Many people also find success by participating in accountability group. These groups allow individual to support each other in reaching their goals and can help keep you on track, share progress and provide mutual support and encouragement. Knowing that others are working toward their goals can create a sense of community and motivate individuals to stay on track.

Replacing Procrastination with Action

One of the most effective ways to combat procrastination is to replace inaction with deliberate action—even if it's just a small step. The hardest part of overcoming procrastination is often starting the task. Once you begin, momentum tends to build, making it easier to continue.

Here are some techniques to help you get started:

• **The two-minute rule:** Using these techniques can be helpful. If a task will take less than two minutes to complete, do it immediately. This not only helps you get small tasks out of the way but also create a sense of accomplishment, which can boost motivation to tackle larger tasks.

• **Time-blocking:** Set aside specific blocks of time to focus solely on a single task. For example, you might dedicate 30 minutes to work on a task without distractions and allow yourself a break afterward. Knowing you only need to work for a limited amount of time can reduce intimidation factor of starting, and once you're engaged, you're likely to continue beyond the initial block.

• **Momentum-building:** Start with the easiest or most enjoyable task. Completing even a small task can create a sense of accomplishment that fuels your motivation to continue.

While healthy striving leads to progress and satisfaction, perfectionism often leads to inaction, as the fear of falling short prevents people from even starting.

15.3 Perfectionism: A Double-Edged Sword

Perfectionism is often seen as a positive trait because it involves setting high standards. However, when taken to extremes, perfectionism can lead to procrastination and stifle productivity.

The Difference Between Healthy Striving and Perfectionism

• **Healthy striving:** It involves setting high standards for yourself and working diligently to achieve them while being flexible and adaptable. It's about aiming for excellence, personal growth, and continuous improvement. Healthy striver's are able to recognise their progress, celebrate their accomplishments, and adjust their goals as needed. They understand that failure and mistakes are part of the learning process.

• **Perfectionism:** It is the relentless pursuit of flawlessness. Perfectionists set unrealistic and often unattainable standards for themselves and others. Rather than focusing on progress or learning, perfectionists become fixated on avoiding mistakes at all costs. This mindset leads to an unhealthy fear of failure, self-criticism, and ultimately, procrastination.

Perfectionism is a double-edged sword because, on the surface, it may seem like a positive trait after all, striving for perfection can drive individuals to achieve great things. However, the downside is that perfectionism can be paralysing. Perfectionists often avoid starting tasks because they fear they won't be able to meet their high standards. This leads to inaction, and tasks are left unfinished.

How Perfectionism Can Lead to Procrastination

Perfectionism and procrastination are often closely linked. The fear of not achieving perfection can cause perfectionists to put off starting a task or completing it. They may tell themselves, "If I can't do it perfectly, I won't do it at all." This leads to procrastination, which is fuelled by the anxiety of not meeting their unrealistic expectations.

Here's how perfectionism can lead to delays:

• **Over-analysis:** Perfectionists tend to overthink every aspect of a task, seeking the perfect plan or solution before taking any action, which lead to analysis paralysis. This analysis paralysis prevents them from making progress, and they end up delaying tasks because they feel unprepared or unsure of the "perfect" approach.

• **Fear of judgment:** They may procrastinate because perfectionists often worry how others will judge their work as inadequate. This fear of criticism can lead to avoidance behaviours, where perfectionists delay submitting their work or avoid situations where their performance might be evaluated.

• **Fear of not achieving perfection:** Perfectionists may delay starting tasks because they fear that their work will not be flawless.

This cycle of fear, over-analysis, and avoidance can make even simple tasks feel overwhelming, leading to procrastination.

Strategies to Overcome Perfectionism

To overcome perfectionism, it's essential to adopt a healthier mindset. Here are some strategies that can help:

•	**Shift your mindset from perfection to progress:** It is important to recognise that no one is perfect, and that striving for progress is more valuable than striving for flawlessness. Focus on incremental improvements rather than unattainable standards and celebrate small wins along the way.

•	**Practice self-compassion:** This is one of the effective strategies that can help perfectionism. Perfectionists are often highly self-critical but self-compassion involves practice treating yourself with kindness and understanding, especially in the face of failure or mistake or when things don't go as planned. When you encounter setbacks, remind yourself that failure is part of the learning process, and it doesn't diminish your worth or abilities.

•	**Set realistic goals:** Instead of aiming for perfection, set achievable and flexible goals. Breaking tasks down into smaller achievable steps and set deadlines that allow for flexibility. By creating more attainable goals, you can reduce the pressure to be perfect and increase your chances of success.

• **Embrace imperfection:** Learn to accept that imperfection is part of life. Deliberately allow yourself to make mistakes and learn from them. Practice doing things "good enough" rather than perfectly. Start small, whether it's submitting to a project that's 90% complete or speaking up in a meeting without rehearsing your words perfectly. The more you embrace imperfection, the more you will build confidence in your ability to take action without needing everything to be flawless.

The Benefits of Overcoming Perfectionism

By addressing and reducing perfectionistic tendencies, you can:

• **Reduce stress:** Letting go of the need to be perfect allows you to approach tasks with less pressure, reducing overall stress.

• **Increase productivity:** When you're not paralysed by fear of imperfection, you can start tasks more quickly and complete them more efficiently.

• **Improve self-esteem:** By embracing progress over perfection, you can build a more positive self-image, as you begin to appreciate your efforts rather than focusing on shortcomings.

• **Enhance creativity:** Letting go of perfectionism frees up mental space for creativity, as you're no longer constrained by the fear of making mistakes.

Chapter 16: Financial Management and Wealth Building

Managing money effectively is a cornerstone of personal freedom and security. Good financial management not only ensures stability in the short term but also lays the foundation for future wealth. In a world where economic changes are constant, the ability to manage and grow one's financial resources is vital for achieving long-term goals and financial independence. However, many people struggle with finances, whether it's due to a lack of understanding, poor financial habits, or simply being overwhelmed by the complexity of the financial world. In this chapter, we will explore the importance of financial management, building a strong financial foundation, and strategies for wealth building.

16.1 The Importance of Financial Management

Why Financial Literacy Matters

Financial literacy is the ability to understand and effectively use various financial skills, including personal financial management, budgeting, and investing. It is more than just knowing how to make a budget or understanding the difference between saving and investing—it's about developing a mindset that enables informed financial decision-making. Financial literacy matters because it empowers individuals to manage their money wisely, reduce debt, and build wealth. Without financial literacy, people often make poor financial choices, like overspending, accruing debt, and failing to save for retirement.

Financial literacy is essential in a society where consumerism is prevalent. People are constantly bombarded with messages encouraging spending rather than saving or investing. Without a solid understanding of how money works, many fall into the trap of living pay check to pay check, despite having good income. Financially literate individuals, on the other hand, can navigate these pressures by budgeting, prioritising saving, and investing wisely. Financial literacy provides the foundation for making informed decisions about everything from everyday expenses to long-term investments, like buying a house or planning for retirement.

The Psychological Impact of Financial Stability

Financial stability does more than just provide a cushion for emergencies it has a profound effect on psychological well-being. The stress of living with financial uncertainty can lead to anxiety, depression, and other mental health issues. On the other hand, achieving financial stability fosters peace of mind and a sense of control over one's life. People who are financially stable are more confident about their future, more likely to pursue opportunities, and less likely to feel trapped in unsatisfying jobs or relationships due to financial dependence.

When finances are in order, it allows individuals to focus on other aspects of their lives without the constant worry about how to make ends meet. Financial stability doesn't necessarily mean being wealthy rather, it's about being in control of one's finances, having savings, and not being burdened by unmanageable debt. This control leads to reduced stress and better decision-making, as financial worries no longer dominate daily life. Research shows that people who are financially stable tend to be happier and more satisfied with their lives, as they have the freedom to make choices based on their desires, not just their immediate financial needs.

The Benefits of Budgeting and Saving

Budgeting is the cornerstone of good financial management. A budget is a financial plan that helps individuals track their income and expenses, ensuring that they live within their means and prioritise saving for future goals. By budgeting, individuals can make sure they are not overspending and can identify areas where they can cut costs. Saving is a natural by-product of effective budgeting. When individuals allocate a portion of their income toward savings, they build a financial safety net for emergencies and future investments.

The benefits of budgeting are far-reaching. First, it provides clarity on where money is going each month, helping to eliminate unnecessary expenses. Second, it forces individuals to think about their financial priorities, whether that's saving for a house, retirement, or simply paying off debt. Third, budgeting allows people to save for emergencies, giving them peace of mind in case of unexpected expenses. Saving regularly also helps individuals accumulate wealth over time. Even small savings can grow significantly with interest and investment returns, especially when started early.

16.2 Building a Strong Financial Foundation

Creating and Sticking to a Budget

The first step to building a strong financial foundation is creating and sticking to a budget. A budget serves as a roadmap for managing money, helping individuals allocate their income towards necessary expenses, savings, and debt repayment. To create an effective budget, it's essential to track income and expenses accurately. Many people are surprised to discover where their money goes when they track every expenditure for a month, whether it's on dining out, entertainment, or unnecessary subscriptions.

Once income and expenses are tracked, the next step is to categorise them into essential and non-essential spending. Essential spending includes rent or mortgage, utilities, groceries, transportation, and healthcare. Non-essential spending includes things like dining out, entertainment, and luxury purchases. The goal of budgeting is to ensure that essential expenses are covered while also allocating money toward savings and debt repayment. The key to sticking to a budget is discipline and reviewing it regularly to ensure that spending aligns with one's financial goals. Automating payments and savings can also help maintain consistency in sticking to a budget.

Managing Debt and Building Credit

Debt management is another crucial aspect of building a strong financial foundation. Not all debt is bad, but uncontrolled debt can be a significant obstacle to financial stability. Credit card debt, for example, can quickly spiral out of control due to high interest rates. It's important to prioritise paying off high-interest debt to avoid accruing more over time. A good debt management strategy involves paying more than the minimum on loans and credit card bills and consolidating high-interest debt where possible.

Building and maintaining good credit is also essential. Credit scores play a significant role in determining one's ability to borrow money, buy a house, or even secure a job. A high credit score can lead to lower interest rates on loans and credit cards, which saves money in the long run. To build credit, individuals should pay their bills on time, keep their credit card balances low, and avoid opening too many new accounts in a short period. Monitoring credit reports regularly can also help catch errors or fraud, which could negatively impact credit scores.

Saving and Investing for the Future

Saving is essential for financial security, but investing is what enables long-term wealth building. It's important to have both an emergency fund for immediate needs and investments for future growth. An emergency fund should cover three to six months of living expenses and be easily accessible in case of unexpected events, such as job loss or medical emergencies.

Once an emergency fund is established, the next step is to invest for the future. Investing allows money to grow over time, helping individuals build wealth and achieve financial goals like buying a house, funding education, or retiring comfortably. There are many ways to invest, including stocks, bonds, mutual funds, and real estate. The key is to start early and take advantage of compound interest, where the returns on investments generate more returns over time. Even small investments can grow significantly over the years, making it easier to build wealth.

16.3 Wealth Building Strategies

Multiple Income Streams and Passive Income

One of the most effective ways to build wealth is by diversifying income streams. Relying on a single source of income, like a full-time job, can be risky, especially in uncertain economic times. By creating multiple income streams, individuals can increase their financial stability and accelerate wealth building. This can include side businesses, freelancing, or creating passive income sources such as rental properties or online businesses.

Passive income is particularly valuable because it continues to generate money with minimal effort once the initial setup is complete. Examples of passive income include investing in dividend-paying stocks, real estate investments, and royalties from creative work. Building passive income streams can take time, but the long-term benefits are substantial. It allows individuals to earn money even while they sleep, providing financial security and flexibility.

Real Estate, Stocks, and Other Investments

Investing in real estate and stocks are two of the most popular ways to build wealth. Real estate is a tangible asset that can appreciate over time and generate rental income. Purchasing property can be a lucrative investment, especially in growing markets, and can serve as both a source of passive income and long-term wealth.

Stock market investing is another powerful wealth-building tool. Over time, the stock market has historically provided higher returns than other types of investments. By investing in a diversified portfolio of stocks, individuals can benefit from the growth of companies and the economy. Stocks provide opportunities for both short-term gains and long-term wealth accumulation through appreciation and dividends.

Other investment options include bonds, mutual funds, and alternative investments such as commodities and cryptocurrencies. Bonds provide a more stable but lower return than stocks, making them a good choice for more conservative investors. Mutual funds pool money from many investors to buy a diversified mix of stocks, bonds, and other securities, offering an easy way for individuals to invest without picking individual stocks. Cryptocurrencies and commodities, like gold or oil, can be riskier but offer high potential returns for those willing to tolerate volatility.

Planning for Financial Independence

Financial independence occurs when an individual has enough income or savings to cover their living expenses without needing to work. For many, the goal is to retire early and enjoy the freedom to pursue hobbies, travel, or spend time with family. Achieving financial independence requires a combination of smart financial planning, disciplined saving, and effective investing.

The first step toward financial independence is defining what it means for you. Everyone's financial goals are different, and the amount needed for financial independence varies based on lifestyle, expenses, and desired retirement age. Once the target is set, individuals can work backward to determine how much they need to save and invest to reach that goal. This often involves aggressive saving, building multiple income streams, and investing in assets that generate passive income.

Reaching financial independence may take years of consistent effort, but the reward is the freedom to live life on your terms. The key is to start early, stay disciplined, and make smart financial decisions along the way.

Chapter 17: Health and Wellness: The Mind-Body Connection

The connection between the mind and body is one of the most critical aspects of overall health and wellness. For centuries, the mind-body connection has been recognised as an essential factor in maintaining a balanced, healthy life. Today, modern science and medicine continue to reinforce the idea that mental, emotional, and physical health are deeply intertwined. Neglecting one aspect of health often leads to imbalances in others, making it essential to nurture both the mind and body for complete well-being. In this chapter, we will explore the profound ways in which mental and physical health are interconnected, how to enhance physical and mental well-being, and the importance of adopting a holistic approach to health.

17.1 Understanding the Mind-Body Connection

How Mental and Physical Health are Interconnected

The interconnectedness of mental and physical health has been the subject of extensive research, revealing just how deeply the two influence each other. The mind-body connection suggests that our thoughts and emotions can create physiological responses in our bodies. For example, when a person experiences stress, anxiety or depression often trigger a release of stress hormones like cortisol, which, if sustained over time, can lead to physical problems such as high blood pressure, weakened immunity, and digestive issues.

This relationship is bidirectional. Physical health conditions also have a significant impact on mental and emotional states. Chronic illnesses, such as diabetes, heart disease, or autoimmune conditions, can cause emotional distress, lead to depression or anxiety, and affect a person's overall mental health. This illustrates how crucial it is to consider mental and emotional well-being when addressing physical health issues.

Recent studies in the field of psychoneuroimmunology have further established that the brain and immune system are in constant communication. When the mind is under stress or anxiety, it directly influences the body's immune response, increasing inflammation and reducing the body's ability to fight off illness. On the other hand, positive mental states, such as happiness, calmness, and optimism, have been shown to boost immune function and enhance the body's ability to recover from illness.

Incorporating practices that promote mental well-being such as meditation, yoga, and positive thinking can positively affect the physical body. Similarly, maintaining physical health through regular exercise, good nutrition, and adequate sleep can improve mental and emotional well-being.

The Role of Stress and Emotions on Physical Health

Stress and emotions play a central role in the mind-body connection. When we experience stress whether from work, relationships, or other life pressures our bodies release stress hormones like cortisol and adrenaline. These hormones are part of the body's natural "fight or flight" response, which is designed to help us respond to immediate threats. However, chronic stress, which occurs when these hormones are elevated over long periods, can have damaging effects on the body.

Chronic stress can lead to a host of physical problems, including heart disease, high blood pressure, weakened immune function, and digestive issues or even cancer. It can also exacerbate existing conditions, such as diabetes, asthma or irritable bowel syndrome (IBS). Emotional states such as anger, frustration, and sadness can intensify stress responses and contribute to physical symptoms like headaches, muscle tension, or digestive problems. For example, people who experience prolonged anger are more likely to suffer from hypertension and heart disease.

On the flip side, positive emotions such as joy, gratitude, and love can mitigate the effects of stress by triggering the release of "feel good" chemicals in the brain like endorphins and dopamine which promote relaxation and well-being. Research shows that individuals who experience positive emotions regularly tend to have lower levels of inflammation, healthier immune responses, and reduced risk of chronic disease. This underscores the importance of emotional regulation and stress management as key components of overall health.

The Importance of Holistic Wellness

Holistic wellness is an approach to health that considers the whole person mind, body, and spirit rather than just focusing on individual symptoms or treating isolated conditions. Holistic health emphasises the connection between mental, emotional, and physical well-being and encourages practices that nurture all aspects of health simultaneously.

Holistic wellness encourages individuals to take responsibility for their health by adopting habits and practices that promote balance and harmony. This includes engaging in physical activities that improve strength and flexibility, following a balanced diet, managing stress through mindfulness practices, and cultivating emotional intelligence. Rather than waiting for illness or discomfort to appear, holistic wellness promotes preventative care and lifestyle choices that support long-term health.

Holistic approaches to health are increasingly supported by research showing that integrative practices such as yoga, meditation, acupuncture, massage, herbal medicine and even aromatherapy can improve both mental and physical health. These therapies can enhance the body's natural healing abilities, promote relaxation, and are often used to complement traditional medical treatments leading to better outcomes for individuals dealing with chronic conditions, stress and emotional difficulties which further reinforce the mind-body connection.

Incorporating holistic wellness into daily life can lead to a greater sense of overall balance, fulfillment, and health. Individuals are encouraged to reflect on how their mental, emotional, and physical health interact and to adopt a proactive approach to nurturing all three.

17.2 Enhancing Physical Health

The Benefits of Regular Exercise

Physical exercise is one of the most powerful tools for enhancing both physical and mental health. The benefits of exercise are well-documented, ranging from improving cardiovascular health, better muscle tone and flexibility to promoting mental well-being. Engaging in regular exercise reduces the risk of chronic diseases, such as obesity, diabetes, hypertension, and heart disease.

Additionally, exercise helps maintain healthy body weight, it also plays a critical role in maintaining bone density, improving respiratory function, and boosting energy levels.

Exercise isn't just good for the body it's also incredibly beneficial for mental health. When we engage in physical activity our bodies trigger the release of chemicals known as endorphins, which act as the natural painkillers and mood elevators. These endorphins are often referred to as "runner high" as they create feelings of euphoria, which help alleviate feelings of stress. Regular exercise also known to boost serotonin levels, which can alleviate symptoms of mental health conditions such as anxiety, and depression. Additionally, engaging in physical activity improve mood, improve cognitive function, memory, concentration and increase overall well-being.

There are many forms of exercise to choose from, including aerobic activities such as running, cycling, and swimming which help improve heart and lung function, while resistance training enhances muscle strength and endurance. Flexibility exercises like yoga, and Pilates promote balance, posture, and flexibility while also reducing the risk of injury. The key is finding an activity that you enjoy and that fits into your lifestyle. Incorporating movement into daily routines, even in small ways such as taking the stairs instead of the lift or walking during lunch breaks can make a significant difference in both physical and mental health.

Beyond its physical benefits, exercise fosters a sense of accomplishment and self-esteem. As individuals set fitness goals and achieve them, they experience boosts in confidence and motivation. Exercise also provides an outlet for emotional release, offering a productive way to cope with stress, anger, or frustration.

Nutrition for Optimal Health

The old saying "you are what you eat" holds a great deal of truth when it comes to overall health and wellness. The food we consume fuels our bodies and minds, and a balanced diet is essential for maintaining good physical and mental health. Proper nutrition provides the body with the necessary nutrients, vitamins, and minerals to function optimally and prevent chronic illnesses.

Eating a diet rich in whole, unprocessed foods, including fruits, vegetables, whole grains, lean proteins, and healthy fats supports energy levels, enhances cognitive function, and maintains a healthy weight. Certain foods are particularly beneficial for brain health. For example, omega-3 fatty acids, found in fish like salmon and mackerel and flaxseeds, are essential for cognitive function and emotional regulation also it helps reduce inflammation in the brain. Foods rich in antioxidants, which are found in berries, nuts, and dark leafy greens, help protect the brain from oxidative stress and inflammation, which can contribute to cognitive decline and mood disorders.

In contrast, a diet high in processed foods, refined sugars, and unhealthy fats can contribute to poor physical health and mental fatigue. Processed foods often lead to energy crashes, increased inflammation, and an imbalance in mood-regulating hormones, such as serotonin and dopamine. This can result in mood swings, irritability, and cognitive decline.

Eating habits also play a crucial role in emotional well-being. Engaging in mindful eating practices, where individuals pay attention to hunger cues, eat slowly, and savour their food, can reduce overeating, improve digestion, and foster a positive relationship with food. Additionally, drinking plenty of water is essential for keeping the body and brain hydrated, which improves concentration, energy, and mood.

Sleep and Its Impact on Wellness

Sleep is one of the most overlooked aspects of health and wellness, yet it is vital for maintaining both physical and mental well-being. During sleep, the body undergoes essential repair processes, from muscle recovery to brain function optimisation. Poor sleep, on the other hand whether due to stress, anxiety, or an inconsistent sleep schedule, can have a range of negative effects on health, including weakened immune function, weight gain, increased risk of chronic diseases, and impaired cognitive function.

Lack of sleep is also closely linked to mental health issues. People who do not get enough sleep are more likely to experience symptoms of anxiety, depression, and mood instability. Sleep deprivation affects the brain's ability to regulate emotions and cope with stress, making it harder to manage daily challenges.

Establishing a consistent sleep routine is one of the most effective ways to improve both physical and mental health. This includes going to bed and waking up at the same time each day, creating a relaxing bedtime routine, and avoiding stimulants such as caffeine or electronics before bed. Aim for 7-9 hours of quality sleep per night to ensure that both the mind and body are well-rested and functioning at their best.

17.3 Cultivating Mental and Emotional Health

Practices for Mental Clarity and Focus

Mental clarity and focus are essential for productivity, decision-making, and overall mental well-being. In today's fast-paced world, distractions are everywhere, like for example distraction from technology, from multitasking, and from stress can often cloud our minds and making it challenging to maintain concentration and focus on tasks. Cultivating mental clarity requires consistent practice and intentional efforts to clear the mind of clutter and distractions.

Mindfulness and meditation are two practices that can significantly enhance mental clarity and focus. Mindfulness involves paying attention to the present moment without judgment, which helps reduce mental distractions and increases awareness of thoughts and feelings. Meditation, particularly practices that involve focusing on the breath or a single point of concentration, trains the brain to become more attentive and focused over time.

Engaging in regular mental exercises, such as puzzles, reading, and learning new skills, can also improve cognitive function and clarity. Additionally, reducing mental fatigue through proper sleep, nutrition, and hydration can enhance mental sharpness and focus throughout the day.

Another key to mental clarity is organising tasks and setting priorities. By breaking down large tasks into smaller, manageable steps, individuals can reduce the feeling of being overwhelmed and stay focused on their goals. Time management techniques such as the Pomodoro Technique or time-blocking can further enhance productivity and mental focus.

Techniques for Emotional Regulation

Emotional regulation is the ability to manage and respond to emotional experiences in a healthy and constructive way. It is a crucial skill for maintaining mental health and fostering positive relationships. Poor emotional regulation can lead to outbursts, chronic stress, and strained relationships, while effective emotional regulation promotes emotional stability, resilience, and well-being.

There are several techniques for improving emotional regulation:

1.   **Mindfulness and Meditation:** These practices help individuals become more aware of their emotions, allowing them to observe feelings without immediately reacting. This awareness creates space for thoughtful responses instead of impulsive reactions.

2.   Cognitive Behavioural Techniques: This approach involves identifying and challenging negative thought patterns that contribute to emotional distress. By reframing these thoughts, individuals can regulate their emotions more effectively.

3.   Breathing Exercises: Deep, slow breathing helps calm the nervous system and reduce emotional intensity. Techniques such as diaphragmatic breathing or the 4-7-8 method can help regulate emotions during stressful situations.

4.   Journaling: Writing down thoughts and feelings can help process emotions, identify patterns, and develop strategies for coping with difficult emotions.

By incorporating these techniques into daily life, individuals can build emotional resilience and respond to challenges with greater calm and clarity.

Maintaining a Healthy Mindset

A healthy mindset is fundamental to overall well-being. It involves cultivating positive thoughts, self-compassion, and resilience in the face of life's challenges. Maintaining a healthy mindset requires a combination of practices that support mental, emotional, and physical health.

One key aspect of a healthy mindset is the practice of gratitude. Regularly acknowledging and appreciating the positive aspects of life can shift focus away from negativity and foster a sense of contentment. Another important component is self-compassion, treating oneself with kindness and understanding, especially during difficult times.

Finally, maintaining a growth mindset, as opposed to a fixed mindset, helps individuals view challenges as opportunities for growth rather than as insurmountable obstacles. A growth mindset fosters resilience, encourages learning, and helps individuals stay motivated and optimistic.

Chapter 18: The Art of Self-Care

Self-care is an essential aspect of living a balanced and fulfilling life, yet it's often misunderstood, neglected, or viewed as selfish. However, prioritising self-care is crucial for maintaining our physical, emotional, and mental well-being. As society becomes more fast-paced and demanding, taking time to nurture ourselves becomes even more important. This chapter delves deeply into what self-care means, how to practice it, and why it is vital for long-term health and happiness.

18.1 The Importance of Self-Care

What Self-Care Really Means

Self-care is a broad concept that encompasses any activity deliberately undertaken to enhance one's physical, mental, or emotional well-being. It's about recognising the need to take care of ourselves to function at our best. At its core, self-care involves replenishing energy, managing stress, and finding balance in life. Contrary to popular belief, self-care is not selfish. It is an essential practice that enables individuals to be more productive, compassionate, and resilient in their personal and professional lives.

In today's society, self-care is often reduced to spa days or indulgent treats, but it goes far beyond surface-level pampering. True self-care involves practices that restore balance and replenish energy. These activities can be as simple as taking a walk in nature, practicing mindfulness, setting healthy boundaries, or making time for hobbies. It requires self-awareness to recognise when we are emotionally, physically, or mentally depleted and need to rest and rejuvenate.

Self-care also differs from person to person. What works for one person may not necessarily work for another. Some may find peace in solitude, while others may feel rejuvenated by spending time with friends and loved ones. The key is to find what nourishes you and to engage in those activities regularly.

The Benefits of Prioritising Yourself

When you prioritise self-care, the benefits are multifaceted, touching on every aspect of your life. The following are some key advantages of making self-care a priority:

• **Improved Physical Health:** Engaging in regular self-care practices like exercise, healthy eating, and sufficient sleep can prevent illness, improve immune function, and help you maintain a healthy weight. Additionally, self-care practices like yoga or stretching can improve flexibility, reduce the risk of injury, and promote relaxation.

• **Enhanced Mental Health:** Self-care is one of the most effective ways to manage stress, anxiety, and depression. Regular mindfulness practices, journaling, or engaging in creative activities can help reduce mental clutter and promote mental clarity. When we take care of our mental health, we are better able to process emotions and face challenges with a clear mind.

• **Increased Emotional Resilience:** By taking time for self-care, we create space to process emotions and release pent-up stress. Self-care allows us to approach life's challenges with greater emotional strength and resilience, enabling us to bounce back more quickly from setbacks.

• **Boosted Productivity:** Contrary to the belief that constant work leads to greater productivity, taking breaks for self-care can significantly improve focus and efficiency. A well-rested mind and body are more capable of tackling tasks effectively. Self-care gives you the mental space to think clearly and make better decisions.

- **Better Relationships:** When you are emotionally and mentally balanced, you are better equipped to nurture your relationships. Self-care helps you show up fully in your personal interactions, enabling you to be more present, attentive, and compassionate. Taking care of yourself also models healthy behaviour for those around you, encouraging others to do the same.

Overcoming Guilt and Shame Around Self-Care

Despite the numerous benefits of self-care, many people struggle with feelings of guilt and shame when they take time for themselves. This often stems from societal norms that glorify busyness and productivity while undervaluing rest and relaxation. Many people feel they must always be working or taking care of others to feel valuable, and as a result, they neglect their own needs.

The key to overcoming this guilt is reframing how you view self-care. Instead of seeing it as indulgence or laziness, recognise it as a necessity for your well-being. Just as you would charge your phone to keep it functioning, you need to recharge yourself to function at your best. Self-care is not a luxury, it's a responsibility you have to yourself and those around you.

Additionally, practicing self-compassion can help alleviate guilt. Remind yourself that you are worthy of care and that taking time for yourself will ultimately make you a better, more grounded individual. Over time, the more you engage in self-care without guilt, the more it will feel like a natural and essential part of your life.

18.2 Self-Care Practices

Self-care comes in many forms, ranging from daily routines to deeper emotional work. While self-care can be practiced in many ways, it is important to focus on physical, mental, and emotional aspects of well-being to create a holistic approach. Incorporating these practices into your routine can lead to long-term improvements in overall wellness.

Daily Routines for Self-Care

Establishing a daily self-care routine can make a significant difference in how you feel physically, mentally, and emotionally. By weaving small self-care habits into your day, you can create a consistent foundation for well-being. Some examples include:

• **Morning Rituals:** Starting your day with a mindful practice such as meditation, deep breathing, or journaling can set a positive tone for the rest of the day. Consider waking up 15 minutes earlier to engage in a quiet activity that nourishes your mind and body.

• **Healthy Eating Habits:** Eating balanced meals with a focus on whole foods nourishes the body and mind. Paying attention to what you eat and how it makes you feel can help you make better choices that enhance your energy levels and mood throughout the day.

• **Exercise:** Whether it's a 30-minute walk, yoga session, or gym workout, regular physical activity is a powerful form of self-care. It boosts endorphins, reduces stress, and improves overall health.

• **Relaxation Before Bed:** Developing an evening routine that helps you unwind and relax is crucial for quality sleep. This might include reading, taking a warm bath, or practicing deep breathing exercises before going to bed.

Physical, Mental, and Emotional Self-Care Techniques

• **Physical Self-Care:** Taking care of your body is fundamental to self-care. This involves more than just exercise. It includes getting regular health check-ups, maintaining a consistent sleep schedule, and taking breaks to rest when you feel tired. Physical self-care also involves listening to your body and responding to its needs. Whether you need to stretch, hydrate, or take a walk, honouring your body's signals is an act of self-care.

• **Mental Self-Care:** Mental self-care is about nurturing your mind and cognitive health. This can include stimulating your brain with activities like reading, solving puzzles, learning a new skill, or engaging in creative pursuits. Limiting negative input such as excessive news consumption or social media is another way to protect your mental well-being.

• **Emotional Self-Care:** Emotional self-care involves practices that help you process emotions in healthy ways. This can include journaling to reflect on your feelings, practicing gratitude to focus on the positive aspects of life, and seeking therapy or counselling to work through difficult emotions. Emotional self-care also includes cultivating self-compassion and forgiveness, allowing yourself to feel and release emotions without judgment.

Setting Boundaries and Saying No

One of the most powerful acts of self-care is setting boundaries. Boundaries allow you to protect your time, energy, and well-being by saying no to activities, requests, or people that drain you. Many people struggle with setting boundaries due to fear of disappointing others or feeling guilty, but learning to say no is essential for maintaining balance.

• **Identifying Your Limits:** To set effective boundaries, you first need to identify what your limits are. This involves paying attention to what activities or people leave you feeling depleted and what obligations or commitments are overwhelming you.

• **Communicating Your Boundaries:** Once you have a clear sense of your limits, the next step is to communicate them clearly and assertively. Setting boundaries doesn't require an apology or explanation. You can simply state your needs respectfully, such as, "I won't be able to commit to that right now."

• **Sticking to Your Boundaries:** It's common to feel pressure to go back on your boundaries, especially when others don't understand or respect them. However, it's crucial to stay firm and consistent. Over time, setting and maintaining boundaries will help you feel more empowered and in control of your well-being.

18.3 Long-Term Self-Care Strategies

Integrating Self-Care into Your Lifestyle

For self-care to be effective in the long term, it needs to be seamlessly integrated into your lifestyle. This requires making self-care a non-negotiable part of your routine rather than something you only engage in when you're feeling overwhelmed or burnt out.

• **Prioritising Self-Care:** One way to integrate self-care into your lifestyle is to schedule it like any other important activity. This could mean blocking out time on your calendar for a yoga class, planning regular breaks during your workday, or committing to a weekly activity that brings you joy.

• **Creating Self-Care Rituals:** Rituals can make self-care feel more sacred and intentional. Whether it's lighting a candle before meditating or listening to calming music while journaling, creating rituals around your self-care practices can enhance their effectiveness and make them feel more meaningful.

• **Listening to Your Body:** As you move through different stages of life, your self-care needs will change. It's important to check in with yourself regularly and adjust your self-care practices accordingly. If you're feeling mentally exhausted, you may need more time for rest and relaxation. If you're feeling disconnected, you may need to prioritise activities that bring you joy and connection.

Adapting Self-Care to Different Life Phases

Life is constantly changing, and so are your self-care needs. What worked for you in your 20s may not work as well in your 30s, 40s, or beyond. As you go through different life phases whether it's starting a new career, becoming a parent, or transitioning into retirement it's essential to adapt your self-care practices to suit your current circumstances.

• **Self-Care During Transitions:** Major life changes can be stressful, and self-care is often the first thing to fall by the wayside during these times. However, it's during transitions that self-care is most important. Whether you're moving to a new city, changing jobs, or experiencing a personal loss, maintaining your self-care routines can help you stay grounded and resilient.

• **Parenting and Self-Care:** For parents, finding time for self-care can be especially challenging, but it's also critical. Parents often prioritise their children's needs over their own, leading to burnout. However, by taking time for yourself, you're not only modelling healthy behaviour for your children, but you're also ensuring that you have the energy and emotional capacity to care for them effectively. Ensuring Sustainable Self-Care Practices

The key to sustainable self-care is consistency. It's not enough to engage in self-care sporadically, it needs to be a regular and intentional part of your life. Here are some tips for ensuring that your self-care practices are sustainable in the long term:

- **Start Small:** Don't try to overhaul your entire routine at once. Start by incorporating small, manageable self-care activities into your daily life. Over time, these small practices will add up and become a natural part of your routine.

- **Be Flexible:** Life is unpredictable, and sometimes your self-care plans will need to be adjusted. Be flexible with yourself and recognise that it's okay to change your self-care practices as needed. What's most important is that you continue to prioritise your well-being, even if it looks different from day to day.

- **Re-evaluate Regularly:** Every few months, take time to reflect on your self-care practices. Are they still working for you? Are there new practices you'd like to try? Regularly re-evaluating your self-care routine ensures that it remains effective and aligned with your current needs.

Chapter 19: Social and Emotional Intelligence

Social and emotional intelligence (SEI) are key aspects of human behaviour that influence our ability to communicate effectively, build relationships, and navigate complex social situations. These abilities not only affect personal success but also have a significant impact on professional achievements, overall well-being, and interpersonal relationships. This chapter explores the nature of social and emotional intelligence, strategies to develop them, and the profound effects they have on our lives.

19.1 Understanding Social and Emotional Intelligence

What is Emotional Intelligence (EQ)?

Emotional intelligence (EQ) refers to the ability to recognise, understand, manage, and effectively use emotions in a positive way to communicate, empathise with others, manage conflict, and overcome challenges. Emotional intelligence encompasses a variety of skills, including self-awareness, self-regulation, empathy, and social skills. It plays a crucial role in how individuals interact with others, handle stress, and make decisions.

The concept of emotional intelligence was popularised by psychologist Daniel Goleman in the 1990s, and it has since gained recognition as a critical component of personal and professional success. Unlike IQ, which measures intellectual abilities, EQ focuses on emotional awareness and how well individuals can adapt their emotional responses to various situations.

Key components of emotional intelligence include:

•   **Self-Awareness:** The ability to recognise and understand one's own emotions and how they affect thoughts and behaviours. Self-awareness also involves understanding personal strengths and weaknesses and maintaining a sense of self-confidence.

•   **Self-Regulation:** The ability to control or redirect impulsive behaviours and emotions. It involves thinking before acting and expressing emotions in appropriate ways.

•	**Motivation:** Being driven to pursue goals with energy and persistence, even in the face of challenges. Emotionally intelligent individuals are often highly motivated and optimistic.

•	**Empathy:** The ability to understand and share the feelings of others. Empathy involves recognising emotions in others and responding to them appropriately.

•	**Social Skills:** The ability to manage relationships and build networks effectively. This includes communication skills, conflict resolution, and the ability to influence and inspire others.

The Importance of Social Intelligence

While emotional intelligence focuses on internal awareness and regulation, social intelligence (SI) involves understanding and navigating the social environments around us. It is the ability to recognise social dynamics, respond to social cues, and engage in effective social interactions. Social intelligence helps individuals read the room, understand body language, and adjust their behaviour according to the social context. It is often referred to as "people smarts" and is essential for building strong relationships, working in teams, and leading others.

Social intelligence includes skills such as:

•	**Social Awareness:** The ability to understand the emotions and behaviours of others in a social context. This includes being aware of social cues, cultural norms, and group dynamics.

• **Interpersonal Influence:** The ability to effectively communicate and persuade others, fostering collaboration and trust within groups.

• **Relational Management:** The ability to manage social interactions effectively, including resolving conflicts, building rapport, and nurturing meaningful connections.

Both emotional and social intelligence are vital in navigating personal and professional relationships. While emotional intelligence helps individuals manage their internal emotions, social intelligence allows them to interact effectively in social settings. Together, these skills enable people to build meaningful relationships, foster teamwork, and navigate complex social situations.

How EQ and Social Intelligence Impact Success

Emotional and social intelligence are critical factors in achieving success in various aspects of life. Whether in the workplace, social circles, or family dynamics, these skills greatly influence how we relate to others and handle challenges.

1. **Workplace Success:** In professional environments, emotional and social intelligence are often more important than technical skills. Leaders with high EQ are better at motivating their teams, managing stress, and fostering positive work environments. Social intelligence allows them to build strong networks and navigate office politics with ease. Employees with high emotional intelligence are more adaptable, resilient, and capable of working in diverse teams.

2.   Personal Relationships: Emotional and social intelligence are essential for building and maintaining healthy personal relationships. Those with high EQ are better equipped to manage conflicts, empathise with others, and communicate effectively. In friendships, romantic relationships, and family dynamics, these skills lead to deeper connections and more harmonious interactions.

3.   Mental Health: High emotional intelligence is linked to better mental health outcomes. By recognising and managing emotions, individuals with high EQ can reduce stress, prevent emotional burnout, and cope more effectively with life's challenges. Social intelligence helps individuals build support networks that provide emotional comfort and practical assistance during difficult times.

4.   Leadership and Influence: Leaders with strong social and emotional intelligence inspire trust and loyalty in their teams. They are skilled at managing group dynamics, motivating individuals, and fostering collaboration. Their ability to read emotions and social cues allows them to make decisions that resonate with others, leading to more effective leadership and greater influence.

19.2 Developing Emotional Intelligence

Emotional intelligence is not a fixed trait; it can be developed and strengthened over time. By cultivating self-awareness, managing emotions effectively, and building empathy, individuals can enhance their emotional intelligence and improve their relationships and overall well-being.

Techniques for Increasing Self-Awareness

Self-awareness is the foundation of emotional intelligence. Without an understanding of one's own emotions, it's difficult to manage them effectively. To develop greater self-awareness, individuals can use the following techniques:

•	**Mindfulness:** Practicing mindfulness allows individuals to become more aware of their thoughts, emotions, and physical sensations. By staying present in the moment, individuals can observe their emotions without judgment and gain insights into how these emotions influence their behaviour.

•	**Journaling:** Writing down thoughts and emotions can help individuals process their feelings and identify patterns in their emotional responses. Journaling encourages reflection, which can lead to greater self-understanding.

•	**Emotional Check-Ins:** Taking a few moments throughout the day to assess your emotional state can help build self-awareness. Ask yourself questions like, "How am I feeling right now?" and "What triggered this emotion?" Over time, these check-ins can help individuals become more in tune with their emotions.

•	**Seeking Feedback:** Sometimes, others can provide valuable insights into our emotional patterns. Asking trusted friends or colleagues for feedback on how you respond to situations can offer a fresh perspective on your emotional tendencies.

Managing Emotions Effectively

Once individuals become more self-aware, the next step in developing emotional intelligence is learning to manage emotions effectively. This doesn't mean suppressing emotions but rather responding to them in healthy and constructive ways.

- **Cognitive Reframing:** This technique involves changing the way you think about a situation to alter your emotional response. For example, instead of viewing a setback as a failure, you can reframe it as a learning opportunity. By changing your perspective, you can manage emotions like frustration or disappointment more effectively.

- **Breathing Exercises:** When emotions like anger or anxiety become overwhelming, simple breathing exercises can help calm the nervous system. Taking deep, slow breaths signals to the brain that it's time to relax, reducing the intensity of negative emotions.

- **Delayed Reactions:** When faced with emotionally charged situations, it can be helpful to delay your response. Taking a moment to pause, reflect, and consider how you want to react allows you to respond in a more thoughtful and measured way, rather than reacting impulsively.

Building Empathy and Compassion

Empathy is a critical component of emotional intelligence, as it allows individuals to understand and share the emotions of others. By developing empathy, individuals can improve their relationships and communicate more effectively.

• **Active Listening:** One of the best ways to build empathy is by practicing active listening. This involves fully focusing on the speaker, asking clarifying questions, and reflecting back what you've heard. Active listening demonstrates that you value the other person's perspective and fosters deeper emotional connections.

• **Putting Yourself in Others' Shoes:** Empathy can also be developed by imagining how others feel in a given situation. Consider how you would react if you were in their position and try to understand their emotions and motivations. This practice can help you become more compassionate and understanding in your interactions.

• **Expressing Empathy:** Empathy is not only about understanding other feelings but also about expressing that understanding. Offering a kind word, acknowledging someone's struggles, or simply being there to listen can go a long way in building trust and connection.

19.3 Enhancing Social Intelligence

While emotional intelligence helps individuals understand and manage their emotions, social intelligence allows them to navigate social situations effectively. By developing social awareness, improving communication skills, and building strong interpersonal connections, individuals can enhance their social intelligence.

Improving Social Skills and Networking

Social skills are the building blocks of social intelligence. Developing strong social skills helps individuals communicate more effectively, build networks, and form meaningful relationships.

- **Effective Communication:** Communication is at the heart of social intelligence. Learning to articulate your thoughts clearly and listen actively are essential skills for building rapport with others. Whether in professional settings or personal relationships, effective communication fosters understanding and connection.

- **Networking:** Building a strong network of relationships requires more than just meeting people, it involves cultivating genuine connections. To enhance your networking skills, focus on building relationships based on mutual respect and shared interests. Being approachable, showing interest in others, and maintaining follow-up conversations can help you create a lasting network.

- **Non-Verbal Communication:** Body language, facial expressions, and tone of voice are all important aspects of social intelligence. Being aware of non-verbal cues, both in yourself and others, can enhance your ability to read social situations and respond appropriately.

Understanding Social Cues and Dynamics

Social intelligence involves recognising and understanding the unspoken rules and dynamics of social interactions. These cues can include body language, tone of voice, and even the context in which the interaction takes place.

- **Reading Body Language:** Body language often conveys more than words do. Pay attention to how people position themselves, their facial expressions, and their gestures to gain insight into their emotions and intentions. For example, crossed arms may indicate defensiveness, while open posture suggests receptiveness.

- **Adapting to Social Norms:** Social norms vary depending on the context, culture, and setting. Being socially intelligent means being able to adjust your behaviour to fit the norms of the environment you're in. For example, the way you interact with colleagues at work may differ from how you interact with close friends.

- **Conflict Resolution:** Socially intelligent individuals are skilled at managing conflicts in a constructive manner. Rather than avoiding difficult conversations, they address issues directly while maintaining empathy and respect for the other person's perspective.

Building Strong Interpersonal Connections

At the core of social intelligence is the ability to build strong, meaningful relationships. This requires a combination of emotional intelligence, effective communication, and social skills.

• **Trust and Authenticity:** Trust is the foundation of any strong relationship. To build trust, be authentic and transparent in your interactions. People are more likely to form connections with those who are genuine and consistent in their words and actions.

• **Mutual Respect:** Strong relationships are built on mutual respect. This means valuing the opinions and feelings of others, even when you disagree. By showing respect in your interactions, you create a safe space for open communication and deeper connections.

• **Emotional Support:** Providing emotional support to others strengthens interpersonal bonds. Whether it's offering a listening ear, giving advice, or simply being present during difficult times, offering emotional support fosters trust and loyalty in relationships.

Chapter 20: Taking Action and Implementing Change

Taking action is the spark that transforms dreams into reality, ideas into impact, and intentions into achievements. It is the essential driving force behind any significant change, personal growth, or accomplishment. While knowledge, planning, and goal-setting provide a solid foundation for success, none of these will bear fruit without the courage and commitment to take the first step and the persistence to keep going. Taking action bridges the gap between where we are and where we aspire to be, making it the single most crucial factor in creating meaningful, lasting change.

This chapter delves into the importance of taking action, strategies for implementing change, and how to sustain long-term transformation in any aspect of life.

20.1 The Importance of Taking Action

Why Action is Key to Success

Every great success story is rooted in action. Whether it's personal growth, professional achievement, or lifestyle change, the ability to take decisive action separates those who achieve their goals from those who only dream. Action transforms ideas into results. It is the force that moves aspirations from the realm of thought to the world of tangible outcomes.

Taking action is critical because:

• **Action Breeds Momentum:** Once you take the first step, the momentum builds. Even small actions can create a snowball effect, propelling you toward bigger and more significant accomplishments. Without action, momentum remains stagnant, and progress is impossible.

• **Action Turns Goals into Reality:** Setting goals is only the first part of success. Taking action is what makes those goals achievable. Many people set lofty goals but fail to take the necessary steps to achieve them. It's only through consistent effort and determination that goals can be realised.

• **Learning Through Action:** While planning and research are important, they cannot replace the valuable lessons learned through action. By taking steps toward your goals, you gain practical experience, encounter challenges, and learn how to adapt. Action leads to growth because it exposes you to real-world problems and solutions.

- **Building Confidence:** Taking action builds self-confidence. As you accomplish tasks and achieve small wins, your belief in your abilities grows. This increased confidence fuels further action, creating a cycle of positive reinforcement.

The Gap Between Knowledge and Action

One of the most significant barriers to success is the gap between knowledge and action. Many people acquire vast amounts of knowledge but fail to apply what they've learned. This gap often results in a sense of frustration and unfulfilled potential. Bridging the gap between knowledge and action is vital for personal growth and success.

- **Paralysis by Analysis:** Overthinking can lead to paralysis, where you spend so much time analysing and planning that you never actually take action. This can stem from a fear of failure or a desire for perfection. While planning is important, excessive analysis can become an obstacle to progress.

- **Fear of Failure:** Fear of failure is one of the most common reasons people hesitate to take action. The fear of making mistakes or facing rejection can hold you back from pursuing your goals. However, failure is often a necessary part of the learning process. It's through mistakes that we learn valuable lessons and gain the resilience needed to succeed.

• **Perfectionism:** The desire for everything to be perfect before taking action can also delay progress. Perfectionism often leads to procrastination, as people wait for the "perfect" conditions before starting. In reality, there are rarely perfect circumstances, and waiting for them can prevent you from making progress.

• **Comfort Zone:** Staying in your comfort zone can be tempting, but it limits growth. Taking action often requires stepping outside of your comfort zone, which can be uncomfortable or even scary. However, real change and progress occur when you challenge yourself and embrace discomfort.

Overcoming the Fear of Action

The fear of taking action is a common challenge. Whether it's fear of failure, rejection, or the unknown, these fears can be paralysing. Overcoming this fear is essential for moving forward and achieving success.

Here are some strategies to overcome the fear of action:

• **Break Down the Task:** Large goals can feel overwhelming, leading to fear and inaction. Breaking the goal down into smaller, manageable steps makes it less intimidating. Focus on completing one small task at a time, which will gradually build momentum.

• **Embrace Imperfection:** Understand that perfection is not the goal. Mistakes and failures are a natural part of the process. Embrace imperfection as an opportunity to learn and grow. The important thing is to take action and adjust as you go.

•   **Visualise Success:** Visualisation is a powerful tool for overcoming fear. By imagining yourself succeeding, you build confidence and reduce anxiety. Picture the positive outcomes of taking action, and remind yourself of the rewards that await you on the other side of fear.

•   **Shift Your Focus to Progress:** Instead of focusing on the possibility of failure, shift your attention to the progress you can make. Celebrate small wins along the way, and remind yourself that every step forward, no matter how small, brings you closer to your goal.

20.2 Strategies for Implementing Change

Once you've overcome the fear of action, the next step is to implement change effectively. Change requires not only the willingness to take action but also a structured approach to ensure that your efforts are sustainable and lead to the desired outcome.

Creating an Action Plan

An action plan is a roadmap that outlines the specific steps you need to take to achieve your goals. Without a clear plan, it's easy to become overwhelmed or lose focus. An action plan provides clarity and direction, making it easier to stay on track.

Steps to create an action plan:

1.   Define Your Goal: Start by clearly defining what you want to achieve. Make sure your goal is specific, measurable, achievable, relevant, and time-bound (SMART). For example, instead of setting a vague goal like "get fit," set a specific goal such as "exercise for 30 minutes, five times a week."

2.   Identify the Steps: Break down your goal into smaller, actionable steps. Each step should move you closer to your goal. For example, if your goal is to run a marathon, the steps might include researching training plans, purchasing running gear, and scheduling regular training sessions.

3.   Set Deadlines: Deadlines create a sense of urgency and help you stay accountable. Assign a deadline to each step in your action plan. This will keep you focused and motivated to take consistent action.

4.   Monitor Progress: Regularly track your progress to ensure you're moving in the right direction. If you encounter obstacles or setbacks, adjust your plan as needed, but keep moving forward.

Building Momentum with Small Wins

One of the most effective ways to implement change is to focus on small wins. Small wins are incremental successes that build momentum and motivate you to keep going. By starting with small, manageable tasks, you gain a sense of accomplishment that propels you toward bigger goals.

• **Start with Easy Tasks:** When implementing change, begin with the easiest tasks. This helps you build confidence and gain momentum. As you complete these smaller tasks, you'll feel a sense of achievement that motivates you to tackle more challenging tasks.

• **Celebrate Progress:** Take time to celebrate your progress, no matter how small. Recognising your achievements reinforces positive behaviour and keeps you motivated. Each small win brings you closer to your ultimate goal.

• **Focus on Consistency:** Consistency is key to building momentum. Even if your progress feels slow, staying consistent with your actions will lead to long-term success. Make a habit of taking small steps every day, and over time, these actions will accumulate into significant progress.

Staying Committed and Consistent

One of the biggest challenges in implementing change is maintaining commitment over time. It's easy to feel motivated at the start of a new goal, but sustaining that motivation can be difficult, especially when faced with obstacles or setbacks.

Here's how to stay committed and consistent:

• **Develop a Routine:** Routines create structure and make it easier to stay consistent. Establish a daily or weekly routine that includes time for working on your goals. When taking action becomes a habit, it requires less mental effort to stay committed.

•   **Stay Accountable:** Accountability can help you stay committed to your goals. Share your goals with a friend, family member, or mentor, and ask them to hold you accountable. Regular check-ins can provide motivation and support during difficult times.

•   **Keep Your Why in Mind:** Whenever you feel your motivation waning, remind yourself why you started in the first place. Reconnect with the reasons behind your goal, whether it's personal growth, financial success, or improved health. Keeping your "why" in mind helps reignite your motivation and commitment.

•   **Adapt to Challenges:** Change is rarely linear, and you'll likely encounter challenges along the way. Instead of getting discouraged, view challenges as opportunities to learn and grow. Be flexible and willing to adapt your approach when needed, but don't lose sight of your ultimate goal.

20.3 Sustaining Long-Term Change

Creating lasting change requires more than just taking action in the short term. To sustain change over the long term, you need strategies that help you maintain motivation, adapt to setbacks, and celebrate your successes.

Maintaining Motivation Over Time

Motivation tends to fluctuate, especially when progress is slow or challenges arise. To sustain long-term change, it's essential to find ways to maintain motivation over time.

- **Set Short-Term Milestones:** In addition to your long-term goals, set short-term milestones that you can achieve along the way. These milestones give you something to work toward in the immediate future and provide regular opportunities to celebrate progress.

- **Reward Yourself:** Positive reinforcement can be a powerful motivator. Whenever you reach a milestone or achieve a goal, reward yourself with something that makes you feel good. This could be a small treat, a day off, or an activity you enjoy.

- **Stay Inspired:** Surround yourself with sources of inspiration. This could include reading motivational books, listening to podcasts, or connecting with like-minded individuals who are also working toward similar goals. Inspiration helps keep your passion alive and reminds you of the bigger picture.

Adapting to Challenges and Setbacks

No matter how well you plan, challenges and setbacks are inevitable. The key to sustaining long-term change is learning how to adapt when things don't go as planned.

- **Embrace Flexibility:** Flexibility is essential for navigating challenges. While it's important to stay committed to your goal, be willing to adjust your approach when circumstances change. Adaptability allows you to overcome obstacles without losing sight of your vision.

•	**Learn from Setbacks:** Setbacks are valuable learning experiences. Instead of viewing them as failures, use them as opportunities to learn and improve. Reflect on what went wrong, identify any lessons, and adjust your strategy moving forward.

•	**Stay Positive:** A positive mindset is critical for overcoming challenges. When setbacks occur, focus on what you've achieved so far and remind yourself of your strengths. Staying positive helps you maintain resilience and keep moving forward.

Celebrating Your Success and Growth

As you work toward your goals, it's important to celebrate your successes and recognise the growth you've achieved along the way. Celebrating your progress not only reinforces positive behaviour but also helps you stay motivated for future endeavours.

•	**Reflect on Your Journey:** Take time to reflect on how far you've come. Look back at the challenges you've overcome, the skills you've developed, and the progress you've made. Recognising your growth helps build self-confidence and encourages you to keep striving for more.

•	**Acknowledge Your Accomplishments:** Celebrate both small and large accomplishments. Whether it's completing a project, reaching a fitness goal, or mastering a new skill, take pride in what you've achieved. Acknowledging your successes reinforces your commitment to continued growth.

- **Share Your Success with Others:** Sharing your successes with others can enhance your sense of accomplishment. Whether it's with friends, family, or colleagues, sharing your achievements allows you to inspire others and create a sense of community around your goals.

Conclusion

As we come to the conclusion of this book, "The Power Within: Unlocking Your Potential for Personal Growth and Success," it is important to reflect on the key lessons and insights explored throughout. This journey has been about more than just acquiring knowledge, it has been about transformation. At its core, personal growth is a journey of self-discovery, empowerment, and continuous improvement. By understanding the dynamics of our thoughts, emotions, behaviours, and external influences, we gain the tools to navigate life's challenges and unlock our true potential.

This concluding chapter aims to encapsulate the essence of what we have covered, revisiting the most important themes while inspiring you to take practical steps to implement these ideas in your own life. You have the tools, now it's time to unleash the power within and take the necessary actions to achieve personal success and fulfillment.

Embracing Your Unique Journey

One of the most important realisations you can have when it comes to personal growth is that everyone's journey is unique. There is no one-size-fits-all formula for success or happiness. You are a unique individual with your own strengths, challenges, and aspirations, and it is essential to honour your path, rather than comparing it to others. This is a theme that has been woven throughout this book, and it serves as a foundational principle for both growth and success.

The self-help strategies we have discussed are meant to be customised and adapted to your personal circumstances. Whether it's building resilience, managing stress, enhancing communication, or fostering emotional intelligence, the tools you've gained can be moulded to fit your needs. A big part of personal growth is learning to embrace imperfection, accept your uniqueness, and craft a vision for your life that is rooted in authenticity.

In Chapter 1, we explored defining self-help and its benefits, and this is where we established the foundation for everything that followed. Self-help is about empowering yourself to take control of your life, make informed decisions, and proactively work towards your goals. The most important takeaway here is that personal growth is not about waiting for external circumstances to change it's about taking responsibility for your development and taking action, even when circumstances are less than ideal.

The essence of this journey lies in understanding that self-help is a tool for self-mastery, not a temporary fix. It requires dedication, reflection, and consistent action. The deeper your commitment to your own growth, the more you'll find that success is not defined by a singular achievement but by the ongoing pursuit of becoming the best version of yourself.

The Power of Mindset

Throughout this book, we have returned time and again to the idea that mindset is the key to personal growth and success. From Chapter 2: Cultivating a Growth Mindset to Chapter 5: Overcoming Limiting Beliefs, the importance of developing a positive, resilient, and open mindset has been central.

A growth mindset allows you to embrace challenges, persist in the face of setbacks, and view effort as the path to mastery. This mindset shift is essential for unlocking your potential. When you believe that your abilities and intelligence can be developed, you open yourself up to continuous learning and self-improvement. You also cultivate the resilience to bounce back from failures and challenges, seeing them as opportunities for growth rather than insurmountable obstacles.

On the other hand, a fixed mindset where you believe your abilities are static will only limit your potential. As we discussed in Chapter 5, limiting beliefs act as invisible barriers that prevent you from achieving success. Recognising and challenging these beliefs is crucial if you want to move forward. Whether it's the belief that you are not good enough, smart enough, or deserving enough, these thoughts will keep you stuck until you consciously replace them with empowering beliefs that support your growth.

You have learned that growth and success require effort, persistence, and adaptability. When you approach life with a growth mindset, you unlock a world of possibilities, where failures are simply feedback and challenges are chances to grow stronger. By fostering this mindset in your day-to-day life, you are setting yourself up for continuous progress and self-improvement.

Taking Action

Mindset alone is not enough. As explored in Chapter 20: Taking Action and Implementing Change, action is what bridges the gap between knowledge and success. You can read all the self-help books, attend seminars, and listen to motivational talks, but without taking concrete steps towards your goals, growth will remain an elusive dream.

Action doesn't always have to be big or bold. Often, it's the small, consistent actions that lead to the most significant changes. Taking small steps towards your goals, celebrating minor victories, and building momentum are all strategies we discussed throughout this book. In Chapter 8: Setting Goals and Achieving Success, we emphasised the importance of breaking down your goals into manageable tasks and staying committed even when progress seems slow.

Consistency is key. Success is rarely achieved overnight. It takes time, effort, and patience. There will be times when you feel like giving up, when doubt creeps in, or when obstacles seem too great to overcome. In those moments, it's important to remember why you started this journey. Keep your vision at the forefront of your mind, and let it guide you through the challenges.

The process of taking action is about learning and adapting as you go. Plans may change, obstacles may appear, but as long as you stay committed to your goals and keep moving forward, you will achieve success in one form or another. Don't be afraid to take risks, try new things, or fail along the way. Every failure is a lesson, and every lesson brings you closer to your ultimate goal.

Overcoming Challenges and Setbacks

No journey of personal growth is without its challenges. In Chapter 10: Managing Stress and Burnout and Chapter 11: Cultivating Resilience and Grit, we delved into the reality that life will throw obstacles your way. There will be moments of self-doubt, frustration, and burnout. However, how you handle these challenges will define your success.

Stress and burnout are two of the most significant threats to personal growth and success. The demands of modern life can often leave us feeling overwhelmed and drained. This is why it's so important to prioritise self-care, as discussed in Chapter 18: The Art of Self-Care. Self-care is not a luxury it's a necessity for sustaining long-term success. Taking time for yourself, nurturing your physical and mental well-being, and setting boundaries are all vital components of maintaining the energy and focus needed for personal growth.

Resilience, as we explored in Chapter 11, is the ability to bounce back from setbacks. It's the grit to keep going, even when things get tough. Resilience isn't about avoiding difficulties; it's about facing them head-on and finding the strength to rise above them. Every challenge you encounter on your journey is an opportunity to strengthen your resilience, build character, and gain valuable lessons.

Grit, as we discussed, is about perseverance and passion for long-term goals. It's the ability to maintain your focus and determination over time, even when the road gets rocky. Grit is what keeps you moving forward, even when progress is slow, or obstacles seem insurmountable. Together, resilience and grit form the backbone of success, they are the qualities that will keep you going when others give up.

Building Stronger Relationships

Personal growth is not a solitary endeavour. As we explored in Chapter 12: Improving Communication and Relationships, the quality of your relationships plays a crucial role in your overall happiness and success. Strong relationships are built on trust, respect, and effective communication. They provide support, encouragement, and accountability, all of which are essential for personal growth.

Throughout this book, we've emphasised the importance of emotional intelligence, active listening, and empathy in building strong connections with others. In Chapter 19: Social and Emotional Intelligence, we discussed how these skills impact both personal and professional relationships. By developing your emotional intelligence and learning how to communicate effectively, you can strengthen your relationships and create a support system that helps you grow.

Relationships are also an important source of feedback. The people closest to you can offer valuable insights into your strengths and areas for improvement. They can help you see things from different perspectives and offer encouragement when you need it most. Surrounding yourself with positive, growth-minded individuals will not only enhance your relationships but also fuel your personal growth.

Maintaining a Balanced and Fulfilled Life

In the pursuit of personal growth and success, it's easy to get caught up in striving for more success, more achievement, more accolades. But true success is not just about what you achieve, it's about how you feel along the way. A fulfilled life is one that balances growth with contentment, ambition with gratitude, and progress with presence.

In Chapter 16: Financial Management and Wealth Building, we discussed the importance of financial stability in achieving long-term success. While financial success is important, it's also crucial to maintain balance in other areas of your life your health, relationships, mental well-being, and personal fulfillment.

Happiness and fulfillment come from aligning your life with your values and purpose. It's about recognising that success isn't just about external accomplishments it's about internal peace and satisfaction. As you continue your journey of personal growth, remember to take time to reflect on what truly matters to you. Define success on your own terms and prioritise the things that bring you joy and fulfillment.

Moving Forward

As we conclude this book, it's important to recognise that personal growth is not a destination, it's a lifelong journey. There will always be new challenges to face, new lessons to learn, and new opportunities to grow. The key is to approach life with an open mind, a willingness to learn, and a commitment to becoming the best version of yourself.

You now have the tools, strategies, and insights needed to unlock your potential and achieve personal success. Whether you're focused on career advancement, improving relationships, enhancing your well-being, or achieving financial freedom, the principles and practices discussed in this book will serve as your guide.

The power to change your life lies within you. You have the ability to shape your future, overcome obstacles, and achieve greatness. The journey won't always be easy, but it will be worth it. Every step you take, every lesson you learn, brings you closer to your full potential.

Take action, stay committed, and never stop growing. The power is within you, now go unlock it.